DYING TO SURVIVE

Rachael's Story

DYING TO SURVIVE

Rachael's Story

RACHAEL KEOGH ∾

Gill & Macmillan

To the two angels in my life:
Senán and my grandmother, Theresa Keogh

Gill & Macmillan Ltd
Hume Avenue, Park West, Dublin 12
with associated companies throughout the world
www.gillmacmillan.ie

© Rachael Keogh 2009
978 07171 4436 5

Typography design by Make Communication
Print origination by O'K Graphic Design, Dublin
Printed by ColourBooks Ltd, Dublin

This book is typeset in 13/16 pt Minion.

The paper used in this book comes from the wood pulp
of managed forests. For every tree felled, at least one
tree is planted, thereby renewing natural resources.

A CIP catalogue record for this book is available from
the British Library.

5 4 3

CONTENTS

'The unexamined life is not worth living'
SOCRATES

ACKNOWLEDGMENTS

In July 2006, at the end of my drug addiction, I got down on my knees and I begged God to bring the right people into my life to help me get my life back on track. My prayers were answered and since then I have had the privilege of meeting some of the most amazing people: without you all I probably wouldn't be here today to tell my story.

So thank you, God, my backbone, because without you to turn to for strength and guidance, I would no doubt be either lost or dead.

To my beautiful son, Senán, who brings so much magic and happiness into my life. You came into my life for a reason and you give me every incentive to be the best that I can possibly be. I love you so much.

To my family: Lynda, Philip, Theresa and John, Laurence, Jacqueline, Jacopo, Marion and Jonathon Keogh. To Declan Connaughton, Jennifer Donnelly, Naladun, Nhamthi, Thu-yen Connaughton and Reuben Keogh. I put you all through hell, but no matter what happened you always believed in me. Thank you all from the bottom of my heart for never giving up hope and for being there for me as best you could. Love you all. Thanks also to my extended family, the Keoghs, the Kellys and the Foxes.

Patrick, I knew you before I ever met you. Thank you for our precious little boy, Senán. And thank you for teaching me how to love. Even through your addiction you were always there for me as best you could. Love you always.

To Michael Mc Loughlin and Roxy. You are forever in my heart and I will never forget you.

To my editor, Alison Walsh. Thank you very much for being so understanding and for all your support.

To Annette, Jimmy and the girls. Thank you so much for all your support. Special thanks to Alan Furlong. You guided me through the toughest part of my recovery and I am eternally grateful to you for that. Special thanks also go to all the staff in Keltoi, especially Pádraig, because you never let me forget my strengths and you supported me in every decision I made, good or not so good.

To my friends, the people whom I truly respect: Neil Arnold (love you always), Val Arnold, Simon Rynn (you have a heart of gold), Alison and Calbach O'Reilly and family. Katriona O'Sullivan (my guru), Declan Crawford, Rachel Dingle, Thomas Farrell, Gary Cunniam, Tommy K, Brendan Magee, Ann-Marie O'Toole, Eoghan Keogh, Valerie Murphy, Paula Valentine, Karen Dowling, Chris Tormey, Wayne King, Angie, Nadine, Carla, Anita, Helen G, Suzanne, Sharon, Ana, Sandra, Debbie, Diarmaid Cox, Jimmy Judge, Brendan Marsh, Yvonne Kinsella, Ciaran Dunleavy, Alice Kennedy and family. I don't tell you often enough but you are the people who inspire me. Thanks for being there.

Special thanks to Fr Adrian and Sister Elvira. You both changed my life.

Special thanks to Narcotics Anonymous and all its members. You know who you are. To NA, I owe my life.

Acknowledgments to the Smith family: Ann, John, Emma, John-Paul, Kathryn, Claire, Jennifer and Glen. Also to Michelle Kelleher and family; and to Edel Hessanan and family.

Acknowledgments to Fr Peter McVerry. Thanks for always believing in us addicts. We need more people like you. To all the staff in the Rutland Centre. To Tony Geoghegan at the Merchants Quay Project, Michael Durkin at Riz and all the staff at Cuan Dara and Georges Hill Step-down Programme. To Dr Brian Sweeney, to Paul Meleady and all the people at Coolmine, Fr Dennis Rafferty (Enfield) and Seán Mc Dermott, my old counsellor, who believed in me when I couldn't believe in myself.

Thank you so much. To Olive, Robert and Geraldine, outreach workers at Domville House. Thanks for never giving up on me. To all those at Victory Outreach. Much respect to all you people. You don't get enough credit for the work you do.

To my solicitor, Fiona Brennan, thank you for always putting up a good fight for me, and for doing such a good job. Also to Michael Brennan of the *Irish Independent* and Petrina Vousden of the *Daily Mail.*

Thank you so much to all who supported me through my early recovery. To everyone who crossed my path and who wished me well or said a kind word. You kept me going. And thanks to those who doubted me or who said I would never get clean, because, when all else failed, you were my driving force.

In memory of Margaret Keogh and also of my old friends Paulie Murphy, Martin Coin, Thomas McBride, Roy Murphy, Martin Carrick, Yvonne Crawford, Sandra O'Connor, Sinéad Kelly, Jeff Moore, Bubbles and Desi Coutin, Paddy Aery, Keith Medcalf and their families. I thought of you all when I was writing this book.

And last but not least, to the addicts who still suffer and their families. This book is especially for you. I hope my story will give you some hope. Because, without hope, what do we have?

INTRODUCTION

My name is Rachael. I'm smartly dressed, a college student and the mother of a gorgeous baby boy. I have everything I want in life: work I like, the support of my family and friends, my son. I'm a normal twenty-nine-year-old, but I'm also a recovering heroin addict.

For fourteen years, beginning at the tender age of eleven, I put every drug I could think of inside my body: starting at teenage raves with hash and 'E', moving on to other pills such as Napps and benzodiazepines, then to smoking heroin and then to injecting it. To fund my drug addiction I did everything imaginable: I broke into houses, shop-lifted and stole from my own family, and I did other things of which I'm so ashamed I have difficulty even thinking about them now.

It would be easy to say that I took drugs because everyone else did. After all, I grew up in Ballymun when drug addiction was rife in the high-rise blocks. Many of my friends took drugs: some only occasionally, others became full-blown addicts like me, spiralling downwards into crime, ill-health and worse. But really, I took drugs to hide my anger at the family I felt had abandoned me and at the emptiness I felt inside, which only drugs seemed to fill. This anger took me to some dark places: to drug squats, to shared needles, to every garda station in the city, in and out of court, and to Mountjoy prison; it took me to nasty people who did me no good and to a side of life no-one should have to experience. My attempts to run from my past took me far away from Ireland and urged me to take solace in whatever I could find to fill the void, even God and prayer.

I sincerely tried to stop taking drugs: I went to detox after detox, had several stints in rehab, none of which managed to break the hold which drugs had over me. It was only when I came to terms with the pain and hurt I'd been running from for so long and accepted just how far I was willing to go to avoid it, that I could even begin to think about my addiction and what it meant to me. And even then I had to be literally at death's door, very little time left to live, my arms mutilated, my lungs clogged with residual heroin, my fingers clubbed from the poor circulation caused by drug use, and with hepatitis C. Only then did I decide that enough was enough.

And then, my prayers were answered. I found a source of comfort and support in Narcotics Anonymous and in their daily meetings, where I met others just like me or who had travelled the road before me, who accepted me and didn't judge me. I found a rehabilitation centre where, in a gentle and non-judgmental environment, I learned to conquer my demons. I learned to find hope in small things, in the mundanity of everyday life, in the little routines which I had shunned for so long. I came to realise that it wasn't the drugs that were holding me back in a life I had come to hate—it was *me*, and only I could change things.

I used to wonder how on earth people could cope with life without drugs and now I know. Life has given me so much since I stopped taking heroin. I stuck with the rehab and remained clean far longer than the six months which I had managed before. I managed to repair my relationship with my family, to build bridges with those I had hurt so badly and who had hurt me in turn. I learned to forgive myself for the past, to love myself. And life seemed to answer me by offering me new friends, new opportunities and the gift of a beautiful baby boy.

Whilst I was at my worst, the media offered me a lifeline and I found myself and my story splashed over the front pages and on the television. I became notorious, as the 'girl with the arms'. Sure, I told them my story for a reason: because I wanted to get clean and could think of no other way, and because I wanted to show just how bad services are for drug users in this country. The reason I have written this book is the same in some ways—I hope that in reading my story, those who know drug users, their family and friends, who despair of ever seeing them recover, will know that there *is* hope and that the powerlessness they feel about their loved one's addiction is normal. Addicts choose to take that first drug, and only the addict him or herself can walk away. But I have also written my story for other reasons: to understand why I became an addict, to forgive myself and my family and to close this chapter in my life, once and for all. To move on, with my son, to a future I thought I'd never see.

Rachael Keogh
13 March 2009

Chapter 1 ∾

THE BEGINNING OF THE END

JULY 2006

It was a race against the clock, as I could already feel the sickness kicking in. Although I was sweating, what felt like a layer of frost was starting to form down my back. I couldn't allow myself to think about the sickness, though. All I could think about was getting the money and getting the gear.

'Are the shops not open late tonight?' I asked my friend Neil, as we dragged ourselves up South William Street.

'No, they only stay open late on Thursdays,' Neil replied, a look of desperation on his face.

Things weren't looking good; every shop we passed had its shutters down and appeared to be closed. Then, just as we were about to give up and start to think of plan B or C, we noticed that the Bag Shop was open. I took a deep breath as I entered the shop, preparing to engage in a game of cat and mouse with the staff and security guards. I knew that in order to make a few quid, we would have to fleece the place. Our gear cost two hundred euro for an eighth—this would yield us sixteen bags of heroin, each containing one hit. Yet, all the stuff here was so cheap, each handbag ranging from twenty to sixty euro: we couldn't get anything less than six hundred euro worth of stuff, as we sold everything in bulk for a third of its price. And that was before we even thought about cigarettes and food.

To my surprise, though, it was as if me and Neil were invisible. With the staff getting ready to close the shop for the weekend, no-one even batted an eye. We left the shop with the stolen bags, sighing with relief—we'd have just enough to get us through the night.

We were roughly about ten minutes away from the flat that we were staying in, when suddenly I heard footsteps from behind and then I felt a hand on my shoulder. 'Sorry, can I stop you there for a minute?'

I turned around, only to be greeted by two coppers dressed in casual-looking plain clothes. My heart sank. I knew we were fucked. 'Well, my friend, how's things with you?' the garda addressed Neil. 'Still doing a bit of shop-lifting, are we? What have you got in the bags there?'

For a split second I contemplated doing a runner, but I knew that my body was too sick to carry me, so I reluctantly opened the bags that contained the stolen goods. 'Ah, would you look what we have here, just as I thought,' said the garda in a heavy Dublin accent. Before I knew it, myself and Neil were being carted off in the Paddy wagon, up to Pearse Street garda station, to be charged with larceny and possession of stolen goods.

Neil tried to make a case for me. 'Would ye not let her go?' he pleaded with the garda. 'She didn't even know that there was robbed stuff in the bag.'

'Sure we know that's not true, Neil,' the garda replied. 'We've been following you for ages. We'll have you in and out in no time.' But I knew in my heart that I was going nowhere fast. I had a couple of bench warrants that they were bound to find. Which meant that I would be kept in custody for the weekend and to make matters worse, it was a long weekend at that. I didn't know how I would survive it.

On arrival at the garda station my personal details were taken and registered, name, address, height etc, the usual details. I was used to the procedure by now—I'd been through it often enough.

Then I was led to this dingy little cell that smelled of urine and disinfectant and the huge metal door slammed closed behind me. I put my head in my hands and cursed myself for getting into this situation again. But all I could do now was wait.

For the next few hours I slipped into my own little world, one where I was unreachable. I could no longer feel the freezing cold slab of concrete underneath me, or the aching pains in my legs and my stomach as my last fix of heroin left my body. I was reliving the time I first met my friend Neil. It had been four years earlier, in the renowned Rutland Centre, a rehabilitation centre for people with all types of addictions—to drugs, alcohol, sex, food or gambling. I had successfully completed my six weeks of intense group therapy in the Ruts and every so often I would revisit to attend a Narcotics Anonymous meeting, held on the premises every week.

'My name is Neil and I'm an addict,' I heard this boy shout from across a room that was jam-packed with recovering drug users. His voice had a feminine tone to it and I immediately assumed that he was gay. I have no recollection of what Neil said at that meeting, but I warmed to his sincerity and sense of humour at once.

My assumption that Neil was gay was confirmed when I bumped into him in Summerhill one day. 'Alright, love, what's the story with ye?' he said, strolling towards me as though he were on the catwalk. He was decked out in a tiny belly top, skinny jeans that made his ass resemble two eggs in a hanky and with nails that appeared to be longer than mine. 'Don't tell me you're scorin', are ye? Ye fuckin' eegit ye, ye were doing so well.' I had stayed in recovery after the Rutland, but for some reason or other I could never get past six months without using heroin: I became so disheartened by my own inability to stay clean that I went back using drugs. And that was it. Myself and Neil scored gear together that day and from then on we became attached at the hip.

I woke from my uneasy slumber to the sound of my name

being called. I jumped up and looked through the hatch in the door. 'Rachael, they're letting me out,' Neil said as he was escorted back to reception. 'I'll see you when you get out, yeah?'

Within minutes, my own door to freedom was open, but only temporarily.

'Well, Ms Keogh, it looks like you'll be with us for a little bit longer. We have eight warrants for you and you'll be up in court on Tuesday. If you need anything, give us a shout.'

'I need to see a doctor,' I tried. 'I missed my methadone today and I'm dying sick.'

'Well, I wouldn't be getting me hopes up now, if I were you,' the garda replied. 'As far as I know, the doctor doesn't give out methadone any more. But I'll see what I can do,' and then he was gone. I resumed my position on the slab, feeling lonelier than ever before, and braced myself for what would be the longest few days of my life.

———

I was dying inside. I knew I was living on borrowed time; I had brought things too far. Too much damage had been done and it would take a miracle to get me out of this one. I was afraid. The walls in my cell were beginning to close in on me and I couldn't tell the difference between night and day. Every so often I could hear activity outside my door. 'Officer, officer, will ye get me a smoke?' The banging and slamming of doors. Gardaí beginning and finishing their shifts. I kept slipping in and out of consciousness. Still no sign of a doctor. After two nights of going through withdrawals, my skin was beginning to smell like chicken soup. This, along with the increasingly overpowering smell of my arms, which were badly infected and rotten from fourteen years of chronic drug addiction, turned my stomach even more.

After tormenting the gardaí to get me a doctor, he eventually came on Sunday night at 11.30 p.m. 'What can I do for you, Ms Keogh?' said the legalised drug dealer, who appeared to be Indian or Pakistani, dressed in thick brown cords and an old-fashioned cream shirt.

'I've been here since Friday and I'm really sick. I need methadone and dressings for my arms,' I replied, shaking before him in my seat.

'Ok, well, first of all, I can't give you methadone, because I don't have any. We don't carry methadone around with us any more. It's far too dangerous; we've had too many doctors getting mugged.' I was waiting for the punch line, convinced that he was having a laugh, but there was none; he was deadly serious.

'Well, you're gonna have to get me something. I'm on ninety mls of methadone a day and I need it,' I said, as I began to panic.

He slowly lifted up the sleeves of my top, which revealed my rotten arms, but he didn't seem fazed. 'Oh, yes, they're very bad. I can give you a couple of Paracetamol.'

I looked at him in disbelief and I could feel a panic attack coming on. I told him I was an asthmatic and he disappeared and returned with an oxygen mask. Whilst he was out of the room, I took my chance to have a nosey through his briefcase, confirming that he wasn't carrying anything stronger than a bloody Paracetamol. I cursed him and wondered why he was even here.

'Rachael, you can take off the oxygen mask now. Go back out to reception and I'll send your tablets around to you, ok?' My head spun as I walked back to reception. What am I gonna do? What am I gonna do? I thought, as I passed a door that led out on to Pearse Street. Suddenly I did a double take, as I began to realise that this could be my way out. The gardaí were only feet away from where I stood and I knew that if I got caught I would definitely get locked up. But I was incapable of thinking of the consequences at that moment. My heart pounded in my chest as I pressed the release button on the door. It opened. My veins filled with adrenalin and I suddenly felt like a mad woman on speed. I

raced out of the station, up Dame Street, desperate to oil my
bones and get heroin into my body.

———

When I opened my eyes the next morning I found myself looking
into the faces of my mother and Neil.

Nobody knew about my escape from the garda station, apart
from my auntie Jacqueline, my mother's sister. Although she was
forty to my twenty-seven, Jacqueline was more like a sister to me
and we shared a flat. It was she who had met up with me the night
before to give me a lend of some money. Jacqueline knew the
extent of my drug use and had witnessed it first hand. She was
devastated by my behaviour, but she couldn't bear to see me going
through withdrawals, so she had reluctantly handed me fifty euro,
kissed me on the cheek and told me to be careful.

That night, I arrived home to an empty flat, not knowing or
caring where Neil was. I just wanted the pain to go away and for
my head to stop racing. But it never did. No matter how many
drugs I used, or how much I ran, I couldn't escape from my own
conscience, my own self-built prison. After fourteen years of drug
abuse, I couldn't live with drugs and I couldn't live without them.
Most of the veins in my arms had collapsed or had thrombosis,
along with those in my neck and my groin, from constant drug
use. This made using heroin an impossible task, but even this
didn't stop me. After many hours of trying to inject into open
wounds, I finally got some sort of relief for myself, knowing too
well that I would have to do it all over again the next day.

My poor mother sat beside me now, looking bewildered, as I
told her and Neil what had happened. 'If you were left on the
moon, ye would still find a way to get off; we can't leave you
anywhere, woman,' Neil said, trying to lighten the mood, as he
always did. But my mother's face told a different story. She looked
as though she had aged ten years and at any given moment she

would explode. She was angry at me for doing a runner, but she was even angrier at the gardaí for not giving me the right treatment. After many years of trying to understand my addiction, my mother had finally come to the realisation that it wasn't because I was morally desolate or incompetent. I had an illness. One that was affecting and rippling through my whole family and needing to be treated immediately. The trouble was, I couldn't get the treatment I needed. All of the treatment centres had lengthy waiting lists—at least six weeks—and the one thing I didn't have was time. I knew that if I didn't get the treatment I needed soon, I would die. Every day I was becoming more and more sick: my weight had plummeted to just under seven stone. I was a regular patient at the Mater Hospital, either because of my increasing number of overdoses, or because my arms were at risk of being amputated. Even going to my methadone clinic was becoming too much of an ordeal.

'Rachael, do you remember I was telling you about that journalist who was interested in seeing the way your arms are?' my mother interrupted my thoughts. 'Well, he said that he would do an article about the lack of treatment and the way you can't get help anywhere. Do you want me to take photographs of your arms and I'll show them to him? All we can do is try. He might be able to help you,' my mother suggested.

'Are you for real? Why would I want to put myself out there to be judged and criticised? I do that enough myself.' Going to the papers with my story was the last thing I wanted to do. Nobody wants to be exposed as a drug addict, especially one with a history like mine. I could barely understand the nature of my own addiction and I certainly didn't expect others to understand. With such stigma and shame attached to drug use, people just didn't want to know. Junkies like me were pushed to the side and marginalised as though we had leprosy. Like some sort of forgotten race.

But, although the thoughts of going to the papers frightened the living daylights out of me, after months of trying to get into different treatment centres and being constantly met with red tape, I knew it was my only and final resort. People's judgments and opinions didn't really matter any more. After all, nobody could hurt me as much as I was hurting myself and I was getting top marks for that. 'Yeah, ok then, I'll do it. I have nothing to lose,' I assured my mother. There and then she went and got the camera, took the photographs and off she went up to the *Irish Independent*.

———

I hadn't moved out of the armchair in my flat since I'd escaped from Pearse Street the previous day. My mother, Jacqueline and Neil kept coming and going in and out of the flat as though they were on some sort of secret mission, whispering amongst themselves and every so often trying to have conversations with me. But I had no idea what they were talking about. I was stoned out of my head on Dalmane sleeping tablets—God knows where I got them from.

My mother came into the room now. 'Rachael, look, you're in the paper,' she said as she placed a copy of the *Irish Independent* on my lap. There I was in black and white, arms held out to the nation, looking like something from a horror movie. It was too surreal for me to take in. The girl on the page didn't look like me. I knew I looked a little bit broken, but I never realised it was this bad.

Over the next few days my flat became like a circus, with a whirlwind of curious journalists and photographers asking personal questions and wanting to take photographs of my arms. I faced a barrage of questions:

'How did your arms get so bad?'
'Is that just from using drugs?'

'What age were you when you started using drugs?'

'How are you feeding your habit?'

I wanted my voice to be heard but I also knew that I had to be very careful how I answered these questions. I was extremely sceptical of a lot of these journalists and I didn't want to be exploited in any way. All that I wanted was to get into a treatment centre and get clean.

I was twenty-seven years of age and I had been in and out of treatment centres since I was thirteen. I had tried everything: religious retreats, locking myself into my bedroom and going through cold turkey, holistic therapy. I had been to Cuba, Texas and Italy in search of a cure for my addiction, but even travelling around the world didn't work. I now know that it was because I had never got clean for the right reasons. It was either for my family's sake, or because I had burned so many bridges and had run out of people to fool and manipulate. I had been given so many chances without having to work for a thing. Every excuse under the sun had been exhausted by me to enable my drug use. People eventually grew tired of my lies and false promises and it was only a matter of time before I was left on my own. Between 2004 and now, 2006, I had been more or less left to my own devices: people got on with their lives and I was the one who was left in the gutter. It was the loneliest time of my life.

But, as difficult as this was for myself and my family, being left on my own was my saving grace. It helped me to realise that, by taking drugs, I was fooling nobody but myself. I could no longer point my finger and blame others for my addiction. I couldn't blame my mother and her decision to leave when I was just seven; I could no longer blame my father and his own drug addiction and the fact that he had never been a father to me in any way; I couldn't blame my grandfather John and the tension his unpredictability caused within the family. Now, I was on my own.

But this time, my family agreed to support me if I was willing to meet them half-way. If I wanted to get clean and stay clean I would have to face up to my own demons and take full responsibility for my own actions. However, in order for me to do this, I needed to come off the drugs first. Something drastic needed to happen—and it needed to happen very quickly.

I had given the gardaí at Pearse Street my grandmother's address in Ballymun, so they had no idea where to find me. My mother was bombarded with calls from the gardaí, insisting that she get me to hand myself in. But my mother refused. She told them that unless they could promise her that I would receive proper medical treatment, she wouldn't give me up. We knew that it wouldn't be long before they found out where I was.

After two or three days of my story being highlighted in the papers, everything became strangely quiet. My mother's phone stopped ringing. There didn't seem to be any further interest in my plea for help. My fears, that nobody would want to know or even care, seemed to be confirmed. I sat on my own in my bedroom, incapable of seeing the wood for the trees, but I was certain of one thing: my next destination would be death, or worse, the Dóchas women's prison. I cried like a baby and fell to my knees, begging God to give me one more chance, promising that I would do my best this time, that I would never hurt myself or those around me ever again.

Later on that night, my mother received a phone call. I could hear her talking and sounding very upset. 'We don't know what to do, Alison. Nothing seems to be working. She's very sick and we really need to get her into a treatment centre as soon as possible… She's with me now. Would you like to talk to her? Rachael, somebody wants to talk to you,' my mother said, handing me the phone.

The voice at the other end sounded friendly. 'Hiya, Rachael, my name is Alison O'Reilly. I'm a journalist at Sky News Ireland. I have been following your story and I was wondering if it would be possible to meet up with you? Your mother was just telling me that you really want to get into a detox centre and we think we might be able to help you. Would you be interested in doing an interview for Sky News? It would be broadcast in both England and Ireland and a lot of people will be watching. So you'll have more of a chance of getting help.'

I couldn't believe my ears. She had to be winding me up. How on earth could something as big as Sky News want someone like me—strung out to bits—to be on their show. It just wasn't possible. Only the likes of Tony Blair and people of high status went onto Sky News. But even then, I knew Alison genuinely wanted to help me. For some reason I felt like I could really trust her. That night myself and Alison spoke to each other for hours and she promised me that she would come and see me the next day to do the interview.

———

'What are ye like, ye lucky little bitch, getting to go on Sky News. Sure we'll have ye lookin' like Christina Aguilera in no time,' Neil said jokingly as he styled and transformed my hair into big tumbling curls.

'Rachael, don't be getting yourself all dolled up. You're not going on the Rose of Tralee,' my mother said, looking at myself and Neil as though we were deranged. God forbid that people might think I looked like a junkie. In my family, we have always prided ourselves on our looks and appearance. Looking good and wearing the right clothes can disguise a lot. And so my arms might be eaten away by heroin, but once my hair was groomed and my make-up perfect, I could pretend to myself that I was Ireland's next top model.

Neil, who was a professional hairstylist, considered himself to be a high-class drug addict as well. He didn't have a tooth in his head, but once he kept his mouth shut, his fingernails well hidden and moisturiser in his hair, he could pass for a normal civilian. As myself and Neil fought over the mirror, my mother rushed around our tiny one-bedroomed flat trying to make it look a little bit presentable and insisting that I stash my drug paraphernalia well out of sight.

Eventually Alison arrived, along with a cool-looking cameraman. She wasn't what I expected, the killer journalist in search of a story. She had shoulder-length chestnut hair and a kind and friendly face. She hugged me as though we were old friends and handed me a Marks and Spencer bag full of posh chocolates and wine. 'The chocolates are for you, because a little bird told me that you loved munchies, and the wine is for your mother,' Alison said smoothly, sounding exactly like someone from Sky News. 'This is Gavin. He'll be filming the interview,' she said, pointing to the cameraman, who looked as ordinary and down to earth as she did. Straight away I felt at ease and comfortable with these people. I didn't feel as though they were looking down on me and judging me. I was ready to drop my pretence and open my heart to them and to anyone who cared to listen. My life was at stake and if I had to humiliate myself in front of the whole world to save it, then that's what I would do.

'Ok, Rachael, just relax, focus on me and pretend that the camera isn't even here. I'm going to ask you a few questions, so just be yourself,' Alison said, soothingly. I looked across the sitting-room at my mother who hovered nervously behind Gavin. She knew by my face that I wanted to do this on my own. 'Right, I'll leave you to it. I'll be in the kitchen if you need me,' she said reassuringly.

Alison proceeded to ask me some questions, similar to the ones I had answered before from other journalists. I didn't feel nervous at first. But then she asked me to show her my arms. This was the part that I had been dreading. Nobody had seen my arms in the flesh except for my family, the doctors and a couple of friends. Even using in front of other drug addicts was shameful and embarrassing. On the rare occasions that I did, no comment would be made about my arms, but I could see them looking at me in horror and disgust.

I pulled up my sleeves, expecting Alison and Gavin to make a sprint for the door, but they didn't flinch. 'What is that on your arms?' Alison asked.

'Well, because I've been using drugs for so long, I literally have no veins left. I have been rooting around for veins and you could easily mistake capillaries for veins. The capillaries are so small that they can't handle the heroin. What happens is, the heroin burns through the capillaries and now I literally have black necrosis all over both my arms.'

'How does that make you feel? Does it make you feel frightened?'

'It does, yeah. I'm terrified of losing my arms,' I replied, as I felt my voice begin to wobble and my eyes well up with tears. Don't cry, don't cry, I told myself, and I attempted to force the tears back down. But it was too late. Once I had started, I couldn't stop. I could no longer see Gavin or the camera in the room; I was no longer conscious that thousands of people would be watching me. It all faded away to nothing. All I could see was this woman who, I knew in my heart, was reaching out to help me.

'I don't want to be using drugs,' I continued as I began to sob. 'I have to go off later on and do whatever I have to do to get drugs. It's like all my morals go out the window. My family instilled a lot of goodness in me. I mean, I'm not a scumbag. I'm a good person.'

'What's out there to help you get through this really bad situation that you're in?' Alison prompted.

'I need to be hospitalised. I rang a few places and I've been told that I will have to go on a waiting list, but if I go on a waiting list, I'll have no arms, or I'll be dead by the time I get in there.'

'Do you really think you could die?'

'I know for a fact that I will be dead. Your body can only take so much and the doctors told me if I continue to use, they will have to amputate both my arms'.

'But you just can't stop yourself?' she asked.

'I just can't stop myself. I'm gone so far and I feel so sick, I don't have the strength to do it on my own. I need help. I know I have the potential to do a lot more with my life.'

The interview ended there and I was relieved. It was as though a great weight had been lifted from my shoulders. The rest of the day became a blur. I lay on my chair and felt as if I was floating and there I stayed until the next day.

———

Or so I thought. My mother's screams nearly gave me a heart attack. 'Jesus Christ, Jacqueline, look at this!' I woke up and saw my mother standing at the end of my chair, staring at me as though I had ten heads. 'Rachael, what on earth did you do to yourself?'

I was completely baffled; I had no idea what she was talking about. 'You're like a bloody ad for Cadbury chocolate.' Suddenly memories of the night before came flooding back to me. Memories in the form of fancy walnut whips, orange delights and chocolate strawberry hearts raced through my mind. I had got up in the middle of the night, craving something sweet. I devoured half of my posh chocolates and fell asleep on top of the rest. Any delusions of being Ireland's next top model quickly went out the window. Especially when I looked down at my feet, which had blown up like two big purple balloons.

'Were you injecting into your feet?' my mother asked, as the blood drained from her face.

'I had to,' I replied, avoiding eye contact with her.

'That's it. You're coming to the hospital with me now. C'mon, get up and get dressed.' My mother attempted to lift me up off the chair.

Neil lifted his head up from where he had been sleeping on the floor beside me. 'What's wrong?' he said in a husky voice, still half asleep. He looked at me with one eye still closed. Then it dawned on him… 'What are ye like, the bleedin' state of ye,' he said as he fell back into his sleeping position. By this stage, my mother was no longer in the room, so I took the opportunity to ask, 'Neil, where's the gear?'

'It's in your arm, love,' he replied.

'It's not. I still had a bit left. D'ye know what I done with it?'

'Check under the chair,' he suggested. I put my hand under the chair and pulled out a one-ml barrel. The heroin was still in the needle, but it had turned to crystal overnight. 'Shit, I'm gonna have to cook this up again.' I could hear my mother coming back into the sitting-room, so I quickly hid my 'works' under my blanket.

'I've just been talking to Garda John White on the phone. I told him that I was bringing you to the hospital,' she told me. 'And as soon as you were a feeling bit better, you would ring him to try and get your warrants sorted out.'

'What did he say to that?' I asked her doubtfully.

'He was actually very nice to me; he said that your health was the most important thing and you're not to worry. When you're ready, you have to hand yourself in.'

I looked at my mother, not believing a word she had said. It just sounded too good to be true. My health 'is the most important thing'—they weren't saying that when they had me in custody, were they? 'They've changed their tune quick enough,' I said to my mother, knowing that something wasn't right.

My mother just smiled and we chatted for fifteen minutes or so. Then suddenly I heard a loud knock on the door. It was a knock of authority and I immediately knew it was the gardaí. I looked at my mother, eyes wide with fear. 'Neil, it's the guards,' I blurted out, as he jumped up, still fully clothed and grabbing his man-bag that was almost like his second skin.

'I'll answer the door. Wait here,' my mother told me and Neil.

'I can't, Lynda. I never went to court the other day. I have a warrant as well,' Neil said to my mother as he ran into the bedroom and hid down the side of the bed. I sat frozen to the spot and held my breath as my mother opened the door to the gardaí.

'I've just been speaking to John White and he told me he would give me some grace to get Rachael better before she handed herself in,' I heard my mother say loudly. 'That's not possible, Mrs Keogh. I'm John White and I didn't speak to you at all. We have a warrant to come into your flat. We're taking Rachael down to the station.'

'Don't you dare try and take my daughter down to the station. She needs to go to the hospital!' My mother sounded hysterical now.

'Lynda, step out of the way or we'll be taking you down as well.'

My mother shouted back, 'You can do what you want with me, but you're not getting into this flat.'

I had no choice but to face the music. I shoved my works, filled with heroin, up my sleeve and walked out, still covered in chocolate. 'Ma, just let them in,' I said to my mother who was beginning to get very upset. She stepped aside and in strolled five gardaí, looking very satisfied with themselves. One of them was a woman, who looked three times the size of me and I knew by her face that she wasn't to be messed with.

'There ye are, Rachael,' the female garda said to me. 'You've been a hard girl to get hold of. You know why we're here. Come on, you're coming with us.'

'You could at least let her wash her face and put some clothes on,' my mother said protectively.

'No, you're coming the way you are,' the garda said, not wanting to let me out of her sight

'She can't go in her nightdress. Just give her a few minutes, it's not as if she's gonna jump out the window,' my mother protested.

'Well, we wouldn't be surprised,' the garda said sarcastically as she walked into the bedroom to have a look around. Myself and my mother quickly followed her, well aware of Neil in his hiding place behind the bed. My mother stood at the end of the bed, barely blocking Neil's feet. The female garda continued to snoop around, then she slowly walked up to my mother and stared her right in the eyes. 'I'm giving her two minutes. That's it.'

'Rachael, hurry up, just throw your jeans on,' my mother said, closing the door behind her and leaving me in the bedroom. Needless to say, the first thing I did was make a dash for my bag of tricks, which included spoons, citric, a tourniquet and everything I needed to have a 'turn-on'.

'What the fuck are you doing?' Neil asked quietly.

'I have to get something into me, Neil. I'm not sitting in that station dying sick again.' My hands were shaking as I put the heroin onto the spoon and tried to burn the crystals down into liquid. Then I wrapped the blood-stained tourniquet around my arm and began to search for a vein.

It was as if my mother knew what I was doing, because she kept talking to the gardaí, clearly in an attempt to buy me time. They were having none of it, though, and before I knew it, my two minutes were up. Bang, bang, bang on the door.

'Rachael, are you ready?'

'Yeah, I'm coming now.' I still couldn't get the heroin into me.

'C'mon, open the door.' I knew that unless they kicked the door in, they wouldn't be able to open it—the handle was missing from the outside, so they would just have to wait. 'I'm just ready, will you give me a chance!'

'Lynda, open this door right now, or we'll arrest you as well,' the female garda said, getting more and more frustrated by the minute.

'Ye'd easily know you had no kids,' my mother retorted. 'Anyway, I can't open the door; she can only open it from the inside,' she continued calmly. Then I could hear the woman trying to pull the door from the top. I realised that I was definitely making things harder for myself with the gardaí. It was bad enough having eight warrants for my arrest and an escape from garda custody hanging over my head, never mind resisting arrest as well. I threw the needle on the bed, resigned to going through some withdrawals. I got dressed quicker than ever before and handed myself over to the gardaí.

Down at the station, the gardaí were delighted to see me. They kept cracking jokes about Sky News and my escape from custody. 'Don't worry, Rachael, we're not keeping you here. You're being brought straight to court, then you can go to the hospital if you feel you need to. Is that ok?' one of them asked me. They were making sure to treat me with respect and giving me no reason to bad-mouth them.

They kept their word and within minutes I was being escorted to the Bridewell district court, sandwiched between two plain-clothes gardaí in a Toyota Corolla. 'Jesus, word travels quick in this city,' one of them said as he stared out the window. I followed his gaze and saw a gang of journalists and reporters, many of whom I recognised, standing outside the Bridewell.

I was swiftly ushered through the back door into what is known as the most unpleasant garda station in Dublin and brought to the women's holding cell. I hadn't been in this cell for six years, but nothing seemed to have changed. It still smelt of musk and concealed dirt. The walls were still free of graffiti. Some people said that was because once you wrote your name on the wall, you were signing your life away and you were bound to end up in prison at some stage or another. But the real reason for the clean walls was because of the constant watchful eyes of the gardaí who would patiently sit in line on the opposite side of the iron-barred gates, pretending to read their daily newspaper while they waited for their prisoner to be called.

It was no surprise to me to see the same old faces, facing the same old charges and with the same old stories. For most junkies, including myself, prison and drugs are a package deal. One comes hand in hand with the other, a vicious cycle from which it is nearly impossible to break free. But a lifestyle that is very easy to get comfortable in. Sometimes prison for me was a refuge from the cold streets of Dublin. A warm place to lay your head, eat well, get your methadone and physically recuperate, only to go back out into the real world to use drugs and destroy yourself all over again.

As I sat in the underground cell I felt a sense of impending doom. Even though I had been in and out of prison since I was fifteen, I really didn't think that I could cope with going back in. I no longer had the energy to wear the hard-woman mask just to survive, to pretend to be something that I'm not. I waited in anticipation until I heard my name being called from the courtroom upstairs, my stomach churning.

————

I stood face to face with the judge on his high bench, who glared down at me over the top of his glasses. He was surrounded by solicitors, gardaí and an army of journalists. 'You may sit down, Ms Keogh.'

Every movement I made was carefully observed and noted by the journalists. I could feel myself rapidly regressing into a childlike state and I just wanted the ground to swallow me whole. I kept my head down as the garda gave the judge a detailed account of my charges. Then my own solicitor, who knew my background really well, proceeded to inform the court of my addiction and the urgency of my need to go in to treatment. 'I am applying for bail on behalf of my client, your honour,' my solicitor stated.

'Well, your honour, given the fact that the defendant escaped garda custody, I am objecting to bail,' the prosecuting barrister insisted.

'Miss Brennan,' the judge addressed my solicitor, 'I am not one bit impressed that your client tried to make a laughing stock of the gardaí by escaping from custody. But I am taking into consideration that she needs medical attention and she will receive that immediately. I am hoping that a bed will become available for her within the next week in the Cuan Dara detox centre, but until then, I am placing her into the Dóchas Women's Centre…'

My heart sank. Going to the Dóchas Women's Centre—the new Mountjoy Women's Prison—was like doing a crash course in criminality: The Dummies' Guide to Being a Successful Criminal. Almost everything I had learned about the streets, drugs and crime, I had learned in prison. I would usually finish my sentence being less rehabilitated and more streetwise than ever before. That was it, I thought. I had no hope of getting clean now.

Chapter 2

THE ROOT OF THE PROBLEM

W hen people ask me how I got into drugs, I can't pinpoint the exact moment. There was no one single incident which set me along that path. I didn't turn overnight from a bright, well-behaved little girl, who always did her homework and loved clothes and her friends, to the damaged young woman I became, full of hurt and self-loathing, unable to see how anyone could get through life without drugs.

When I was in recovery that final time, I realised that I couldn't blame my mother or my father or my past for my addiction, but I could understand how they affected me and how, slowly and inevitably, the feelings of rejection I experienced turned into a hatred for myself that I would do anything to conceal, taking more and more drugs to dampen down my true feelings.

It's almost a cliché, but what is certainly true is that many of my problems had their roots in my childhood and in a broken family. It seems obvious to me now, but I only really realised the depth of my hurt for the first time when, back in the Dóchas Centre, a psychiatrist called Dr Sweeney came to see me. Head Psychiatrist at the Trinity Court methadone programme, I had met him many times before and I knew that he was my one and only ticket to freedom. So when he came to see me that morning in July 2006, I was prepared to be on my best behaviour. What I wasn't prepared for was the journey on which our conversation would take me.

——

'Good morning, Ms Keogh. So you have managed to land yourself in here again. What has you in here this time?' Dr Sweeney asked in his elegant accent. He was a short man with receding silver hair and his bones seemed to protrude through his classy black suit.

'Ah, I was arrested for shop-lifting.'

The doctor sat coolly, with his legs crossed. 'Take a seat,' he said, as he signalled to the chair opposite him. 'Now, Rachael, I have been asked to do an assessment with you, so if you don't mind, I will need you to answer some questions. The questionnaire isn't that intense. I'm sure you've done something like it before.'

'Yeah, I was in the Rutland Centre,' I replied. I had answered the standard questions about my home and family so many times before, I had lost count.

'Oh, well then, this should be easy for you,' he said with a smile. 'When were you in the Rutland?'

'I was there twice, first in nineteen ninety-six and again in two thousand and two.'

'So what's so different this time round?'

'A lot,' I replied. 'First of all, I'm older. I think that if I don't get clean now, I never will. I've been clean before, so I know what to expect and I know what I need to do. I haven't used heroin since I came in here, so I really need to go into detox and get help with coming off the methadone.'

'Ok, let's get started,' he said as he opened his black leather briefcase and took out a file. 'What's your mother's name?'

'Lynda Keogh.'

'Your father's?'

'Con Geraghty.'

'Tell me about them.'

'Where do I start?' I shifted uneasily in my chair.

'From the beginning,' the doctor replied, smiling.

Ah no, I thought to myself. He was asking me to tell him in

detail about my life. My heart sank at the idea of an assessment this intense. Even though I knew my life depended on it, I felt that I couldn't face the past just yet, not now. But I was eager for the doctor to know how serious I was, so I did as he said. Looking back on this split-second decision now, I think it probably saved my life. I had had many opportunities to talk about all this stuff before, but for some reason I couldn't. I had been afraid of re-living my past: I thought that looking back would finish me off altogether. But of course my past never left me. It was with me every day, manifesting itself in different ways, refusing to be buried under a tonne of drugs, like some sort of living poison that was killing me anyway. I was afraid, but I was ready to tell my truth.

'Well, I was born in the Rotunda hospital, on the fourteenth of October nineteen seventy-nine,' I began. 'My mother was only a kid herself when she had me—she was only fifteen. My da was nineteen, but he wasn't there for the birth. My grandparents didn't approve of him. Especially my grandfather and he made my mother's life a hell on earth for getting pregnant so young.'

'What are your grandparents' names?' the doctor interrupted, as he made a note of everything that I said.

'John and Theresa Keogh. They practically raised me in Ballymun. They had five children: my auntie Marion, my uncle Jonathon, then my mother, my auntie Jacqueline and my other uncle, Laurence. They are all like my brothers and sisters. There's two years between each of them, so they aren't that much older than me. My mother hid her pregnancy up until the very end. She was terrified of my grandfather finding out.'

'Why?' asked the doctor.

'John wasn't and still isn't the easiest man to live with,' I admitted. 'He was a great lover of the drink. He was built like a tank, with hands like big shovels. He worked as a butcher and made a lot of money. My mother used to joke that they were the first kids in Ballymun to have Barbies with rabbit-fur coats. My grandmother had various jobs, but she was heavily reliant on John financially. He was the boss of the house and what he said, went. They constantly lived in fear of John. He was the type of man who was really unpredictable and chaotic, who would tell you exactly what he thought of you.' I paused now to think of John and his unpredictable moods. My aunts and uncles lived in fear of him and, as a child growing up with them, so did I. But at the same time I loved him dearly, and when he was in a good mood we would talk about everything.

'Every day, he would come home from work, after spending most of his wages on drink and he would wreck the place,' I said, remembering how he might punch his fist through the wall or door. 'For some reason, even before I was born, my mother would get the worst of it. He would call her terrible names, telling her that he would cut her from her neck down to her stomach and bury her in the mountains.' I continued, 'No matter what my family did, John would find something to give out about. If they tried to be quiet he would accuse them of sneaking around the house and of being up to no good. If they made noise he would accuse them of trying to annoy him. There was no winning with him.

'My mother knew that there would be war when John found out about her pregnancy. She was right. After putting up with years of mental abuse, my mother finally found the courage to leave my grandparents' house. Herself and my da got a one-bedroomed flat together in Coultry Road. But she went from one bad situation to another…' I finished.

'What are your memories of growing up?' Dr Sweeney asked softly, already knowing that my memories couldn't have been good.

'My very first memory was when I was just two years old. I was in the kitchen of our flat. I could hear my ma and da arguing. I didn't know why they were fighting or what they were even saying. All that I knew was that my mother was in trouble. The

shouts became louder and louder and I remember having a sense
of panic. Then I heard a bang and a shuffling noise coming up the
hall and into the kitchen. Then I saw my father, his face distorted
with anger. He was bent over my ma like a mad man. He had a
firm hold on her long blonde hair. She twisted and turned, doing
her best to escape his grip. But she couldn't. My ma must have
been cooking something on the grill, because when my da opened
the cooker I could see that the bars on the inside were scorching
red. Then my da dragged my ma over to the cooker and shoved
her head into the grill. Her high-pitched screams paralysed me to
the spot and that's my first memory.'

I took a deep breath and looked at the doctor, who sat
expressionless and unfazed.'Jesus, I don't know where all that
came from,' I said, shaking my head, genuinely surprised by my
own honesty.

'You're doing really well, Rachael. Let's keep going,' he replied.
'Can you remember your next memory?'

'It doesn't get much better, Dr Sweeney.'

'Keep going,' he urged.

'Well, it was around the same time, because we were still living
in the flat. I remember being in my cot in the sitting-room. The
flat seemed dark and empty, as if there was no furniture in it.
Again, my ma and da were arguing. I could hear them shouting in
the kitchen. Then I saw them. They were standing just feet away
from me, in the hall. My da had my ma by the hair. He started to
viciously bang her head off the wall. Then they were out of my
sight, but I could still hear the bangs echoing all over the flat. I was
later to learn that my da went mad because my mother had
bought me a new pram without telling him. Seemingly he was
furious because he needed the money for other things. He ended
up throwing my new pram over our balcony, from the fifth floor.
But I don't remember this. I just remember the violence, because
it really shook me up.'

The doctor nodded sympathetically.

'That was the last time I saw my father. That night my mother left him and she went and stayed with a friend of hers. She didn't want my grandparents to see her bruises, but when my mother's friend saw her, she was so upset that she stormed over to my grandparents and she told my grandmother exactly what had happened.

'My grandmother was at her wits' end, so herself and her sister went over to our flat in Coultry and took all of our stuff back to her house. John wasn't one bit impressed. The last thing he wanted was a seventeen-year-old girl with a two-year-old under the same roof as him. He made it impossible for my mother to stay in his house. My grandmother's loyalties lay with my mother. She wasn't prepared to leave her on her own again, so they took their bare essentials and walked from Ballymun to Finglas in the middle of the night. There they stayed for a few days, with my grandmother's sister, in the hope that John would cool down and come around to the idea of us living there. He did, but he never made it easy. At one stage the mental torture became too much, the name-calling and the shouting, and my nanny, my mother and I had to leave the house for three months just to keep out of his way.'

There was a long silence between myself and the doctor. 'Would you like a glass of water?' he asked kindly as he stood up from his seat and walked towards the door. 'Please, yeah,' I replied. And then he was gone. I sat silent and alone in the assessment room. The sun was shining through the window and every so often I would see the other inmates walk past in twos and threes, as they did their laps around the prison. I looked at my watch and realised that I had been telling the doctor my story for the past half hour. I also realised that in telling my story I felt absolutely no emotion. I was numb and was talking about myself as if I were somebody else.

The door opened and Dr Sweeney came back in. He handed me a glass of chilled water and resumed his position in his chair.

'Ok, Rachael, these must have been really difficult experiences for you. How did they affect you growing up?'

I prepared to continue with my story. 'They didn't really, not in the beginning. I took everything in my stride. I loved living with my grandparents and I used to follow John everywhere. I grew to adore him and he grew to adore me. I quickly learned when to stay out of John's way, though, and it wasn't long before he began to see me as one of his own daughters.

'When I was five years old my family sent me to the Holy Spirit Girls' School in Ballymun. I'll never forget my first day. As always, my mother dressed me in the best of clothes. She had me wearing this knitted powder-blue beret with a shoulder bag to match. On the front of the bag there was this little doll with curls in her hair. My own hair was baby blonde and had grown right down my back and my mother would always put rags in my hair, so it would have falling curls. That day I felt like the little doll on my bag and I was delighted to be starting school. That was until I got there. Every other girl in my new class was crying and didn't want their mothers to leave them, so I started to cry as well, holding on to my grandmother's hand for comfort.

'Then I noticed this girl across the room. It was as if I was looking at myself in a mirror. She wore the exact same hat and bag, but hers was in pink. Her hair was like a golden sun, with big huge curls in it. It turned out that her mother and my grandmother knew each other and they only lived a few doors away from us. Her name was Mary and from that day onwards we were to become the best of friends. We were like two bubbly little angels who never caused any trouble. We both excelled in our school work. Then we would walk home together, get changed out of our uniforms and do our homework before we would even think about going out to play.'

'When did things go wrong?' asked the doctor.

'A lot of things happened before I started to use drugs. I was very sick as a kid. I suffered with chronic asthma, and Temple

Street hospital became like my second home. My doctor, Professor Gill, told me that I should have been in the Book of Records for the amount of time that I spent in hospital. I loved being in hospital, because I would be spoilt rotten and I got loads of attention from everybody. Nearly every night, depending on how well I was, the nurses would bring me down to their staff room. They knew how much I wanted to be a nurse as well, so they would dress me up in their uniforms. Then we would laugh and joke around as I pretended to be one of them. Every day someone from my family would come and visit me. When my aunties and my mother came they really pampered me. They would bring me up these amazing pyjamas, dressing-gowns and slippers, all in different styles and colours.

'My auntie Marion, who was the eldest of my mother's brothers and sisters, always brought along books for me to read. Then she would sit with me and do spelling tests, making sure that I pronounced every word perfectly, as my mother and auntie Jacqueline would do my hair in plaits or curls. Sometimes John would visit me in the hospital. He would try to show me how to play dominos, then he would test my general knowledge, asking me questions like, What's the largest organ in the body? or, What bird lays the largest egg?

'My grandmother would spoil me the most, bringing me up loads of toys, every type of Barbie that was going. When I was sick I really felt like a princess. This wasn't the case when I was at home.

'I think my realisation that, when I was "sick" in some way I would get the attention I craved, stems from this time. Even though I had everything that I needed materially, the people in my family weren't around much when I was younger. My grandmother had started a job as a cleaning lady in Dublin Airport and she worked for the best part of the day. My mother, aunties and uncles were at the age of going out and socialising with their friends. I was left on my own with John who, although

I loved him, could be unpredictable at the best of times. Every day when I came home from school I would say a little prayer that John would be either in a good mood or gone out.'

I continued to tell Dr Sweeney… 'His drinking and his mood swings had become so bad that my friend Mary wouldn't come near our house. This led to me staying with another neighbour who became my unofficial babysitter. I hated being in her house, because it was cold and it smelt of old musk, but anything was better than staying with John.' I cringed now as the disturbing memories of that house came back to me.

'She had a brother who was in his late teens and who always seemed a bit strange to me. He was tall and skinny, with brown greasy hair and pasty white skin. He didn't seem to have any friends of his own and he spent most of his time hanging around his sister. One day he asked me if I wanted to learn how to play the keyboard. When I agreed, he brought me up to his bedroom and shut the door. I was so in awe of the size of the keyboard and of all its gadgets that I immediately ran over and started to play with it. He didn't join me. Instead, he took out a blindfold and asked me if I wanted to play a game of blind man's bluff…'.

As if he sensed the direction in which my recollections were going, Dr Sweeney broke in to my thoughts. 'Sorry for interrupting you, Rachael, but before you go any further I just want to remind you, in the nicest way possible of course, that I am not here to counsel you. I am merely here to assess you. You are doing really well and being completely open and you can continue if you like. But I just wanted to remind you that I won't be giving feedback on what you are telling me. I am more than willing to listen to you, if you want to go on.'

I was revealing myself and my life to this man whom I didn't even know. Everything was coming out and it was as though I had no control over what I was saying. Somehow I knew that I had to keep going. 'Yeah, I'll keep going if that's ok?'

'Sure,' he replied, nodding.

'Where was I?'

'You were saying that this guy wanted you to play blind man's bluff.'

'Oh yeah, he asked me to play a game with him, but I had no idea what he was talking about. He explained to me that I needed to put the blindfold on. Then he would hide and I had to find him. So I let him blindfold me. Then I blindly walked around his room, arms stretched out in front of me, excitedly trying to find him. Then I felt him and he took me by the hand to steady me on my feet. He lifted the blindfold from my head and when my vision became clear I realised that his jeans and his underwear were down around his ankles. I didn't know what was going on. Then, without saying a word, he put my hand on his penis and slowly showed me how to masturbate him. I did what he wanted, but something within me knew that what we were doing was wrong. He kept his hand on my hand as I touched him, then he suddenly jumped away from me. He quickly pulled up his jeans and before I knew it his sister was standing behind me. She had a puzzled look on her face. She asked us if everything was ok and then she left us on our own again.'

'What age were you when this happened?' asked the doctor.

'I was only seven.'

'Did it ever happen again?'

'I don't think so. If it did, I can't remember. But I have memories that don't add up or make sense. I remember being in his bedroom another time. I was hiding under his bed. I was really afraid and I vividly remember the bedclothes. They were like corduroy with strings hanging from the ends of them. I was sitting in the dark and I could just see the light from the hall coming in around the edges of the door. I have no idea what I was doing there. I just know that I was scared stiff. I couldn't even tell you how long that girl baby-sat me for. I think I have a lot of it blocked out.

'It was around this time that things began to change in my

house. My mother was becoming more and more distant from me and I was starting to really miss her being around. At the time she was doing part-time modelling and at the best of times the closest that I could get to her was by wearing her clothes. She would keep these fancy dresses that she got from modelling out in my grandparents' shed. Every so often I would go out to the shed on my own and dress up in her clothes.

'Then one day, herself and my auntie Jacqueline were talking in the kitchen. Jacqueline took out this bag of baby clothes. "They're gorgeous," Jaqueline told my mother, oohing and ahhing over the tinyness of them. I listened and watched them carefully, wondering who they belonged to. I asked my mother who they belonged to, but she just told me that they belonged to a friend. A few months later my brother Philip was born. I had had no idea that she was even seeing someone, not to mind expecting another baby.'

'Your mother had another baby?' the doctor said, looking surprised.

'Yeah, but at this time I didn't even know who the father was. What I do know is that when Philip was born I felt like my world fell down around me. It was September 1986. Christmas was coming and I remember auntie Marion's boyfriend, Declan, being in my grandparents' house. He was dressed up in a Santa Claus suit and was trying to distract me from something, but his attempts to amuse me had no effect. I was more concerned with my mother and couldn't help but wonder why she was pulling all of her clothes out of the wardrobe and putting them into suitcases.

'Declan kept trying to distract me, sitting me on his knee, asking me what I wanted for Christmas. I kept worming my way away from him every time. I couldn't get close enough to my mother to ask her where she was going. Then she came down the stairs with her suitcases and bags. Declan grabbed me and held me tight in his arms. I called after her, screaming and crying, but she looked straight ahead and just kept walking. That was the night my mother left me.'

———

I continued telling Dr Sweeney… 'I don't think that I ever got over it. I cried every night for weeks after she left. Until one day, I didn't cry any more. Of course I have spoken to my mother about this and asked her why she left. She has said that she felt I was better off in the stability of my grandparents' home, in my school and with all my friends. But I have always felt the reasons were more complicated than that. I know now that she had met someone new and so perhaps she wanted to start again, away from her own past—I was a constant reminder of that past. And she was so young, hardly more than a child herself when she had me. But to me, as a seven-year-old, she had simply abandoned me.

'Don't get me wrong,' I continued. 'She still came up to see me every week, bringing Philip along with her. Philip was so tiny and cute. I couldn't believe that he was my brother. But I never got to spend enough time with him to be able to bond with him. I felt like I was outside the window, looking in on my own family. I just thought that my mother would always be there, so when she moved out with Philip, I was really hurt. I was convinced that I had done something wrong.'

'Did you ever tell your mother this?' asked the doctor.

'No, I couldn't. I didn't know how to. God forbid that you express your feelings in my house. In my family, we were experts at burying our feelings. We had learned this from many years of living with John, trying to keep out of his way and not make too much of a fuss. When my mother left, it was no different. Nobody said anything. No-one tried to explain to me what had happened and why.

'So I just kept everything in and pretended that it hadn't

happened. I engrossed myself in my school work and my friends. Anyway, my Holy Communion was coming up and I was really looking forward to it. Religion was one of my favourite subjects, and I loved going to the church to practise our readings for our big day. I couldn't wait for my family to see me singing in the choir.

'It was a few days before my Communion and our families were asked to come to the church for rehearsals. My grandmother came, but during the whole mass I kept looking at the door to see if my mother was coming. She never turned up. When the mass was over, the priest asked myself and all my classmates to kiss our parents on the cheek. Everyone did, except for me. I felt so angry with my mother that I couldn't even look at my grandmother. Again, I kept it all in.'

At this point in our conversation, the ringing of Dr Sweeney's phone brought me back to reality. 'Excuse me, Rachael, I need to answer this.' Then Dr Sweeney looked at his watch. 'We've just gone over time. If it's alright with you, I'll come back and continue the assessment with you tomorrow.'

Thank God, I thought to myself. I was starting to get really tired and agitated. I had enough of talking about myself and badly needed some air. 'Yeah, that's grand, thanks very much,' I said, relieved that, for today, it was all over.

'Take it easy. You have talked about a lot today.'

'I will,' I said. 'See you tomorrow.' I shook his hand and left the room. The numbness which I had felt earlier had now been replaced by a jittery feeling, a churning in my stomach. I had remembered things that I really didn't want to remember, ever. I had forgotten the rage and anger that I had felt against everyone, most of all my mother. And how I wanted to destroy everything. Now the memories came flooding back and I felt restless, uneasy and apprehensive.

The next day I continued telling Dr Sweeney my story. He hadn't forgotten anything.

'Right,' he said confidently. 'We're going to pick up from where we left off yesterday, if that's ok with you?'

'Yeah, that's fine,' I agreed, determined to keep going.

'You were talking about your mother leaving you and of how she never turned up for your Communion rehearsals. Did you spend time with her at all after that?'

'I did, but very rarely. I began to get really resentful towards my ma: I don't think I was even aware of it at that time. Sometimes she would collect me from my nanny's and she would bring me into town. Then she would buy me a knickerbocker glory ice-cream and we would take a walk up to St Stephen's Green. I was completely in awe of my mother. She was so young and beautiful. She had a charismatic personality that everyone wanted a piece of. Especially me. I remember wanting to be like her, imitating everything that she did. That sounds messed up, doesn't it?' I asked Dr Sweeney. 'The more I talk about the relationship that I had with my ma, the more I'm realising just how fucked up I was. Do you think my relationship with my mother was dysfunctional, even when I was that young?' I asked the doctor.

'Well, I think only you can answer that, Rachael,' he answered, giving nothing away. I continued. 'I think I just craved my mother's love and attention. But at that time I was so confused. I didn't know what was going on and I didn't have anyone that I could really talk to.

'I remember this other time, my mother was bringing me up to my cousin Martina's house in Finglas. Martina was a year younger than me and she was celebrating her birthday. My ma had bought me a whole new outfit. I thought that I was gorgeous and I couldn't take my eyes off my shoes. They were little black pumps with bright blue and white sparkles all over them. My mother was walking ahead of me as I trailed behind. I was singing to myself, in my own little world, fascinated with how the sun reflected off my shoes. Then I heard somebody call my name. I looked around me, but there was nobody there.

'"Rachael," I heard again, louder this time. There was no-one around except for this man who was standing in a garden, just across the road. He was in his late twenties with dark hair and good looks. He wore blue jeans and a white vest top. It looked as if he was doing some gardening, because he had a shovel in his hand. He started to wave at me. I looked to my mother to see if she knew who he was. But she hadn't even noticed; she was still walking ahead. Then he stuck out his tongue at me and began to smile. I recognised him from somewhere, but I couldn't remember how or where. I smiled back at him, feeling as though I knew him well.

'"Rachael, don't look at that man," my mother suddenly shouted as she came running back to me. "Let's go," she said, as she grabbed me by the hand and pulled me onwards. I couldn't stop looking at him as he waved me goodbye. The story does have a point, Dr Sweeney, but it wasn't until months later that I realised what it was.'

'Sorry, Rachael, you have just lost me. How do you mean?' asked the doctor, with a confused look on his face.

'Well, my grandmother used to have this big black briefcase that she kept all her photos in…' I continued, recalling the time when, one day, a few months after I had seen the man, out of boredom I decided to have a look through the briefcase. There were pictures of John when he was a fisherman, looking windswept and proud of the fish he had caught. There were pictures of Laurence and Jonathon with their arms around these two girls, looking coy, in Holyhead. There were loads of pictures of my mother and my aunties with the bad perms that were stylish at the time. But one picture stood out to me. It was a picture of my christening. I recognised everyone in the photo, except for the man who was holding me. Then I remembered. It was the man who was smiling at me in Finglas. But I still didn't know who he was.

'Clutching the photo in my hand, I ran downstairs to my grandmother, who was sitting in the sitting-room watching television. "Ma," I called her (I had taken to calling her Ma), 'who's that?' I handed her the photo.

Her jaw dropped. 'Come over here and sit down beside me,' she said, patting the chair next to her. 'That's your father,' she said softly.

'Is it?' I said, taking the photo from her and examining my father carefully.

'But he's not around any more,' she continued.

'Why not?' I asked.

'He's dead, Rachael.'

Then I was really confused. 'He's not dead, because I saw him a while ago,' I told my grandmother, on the verge of crying. I had no idea who my father was, but I didn't want him to be dead.

'When did you see him?' she asked.

'When I was going to Martina's birthday party. He was in somebody's garden beside Martina's house.'

'That couldn't have been him. He died a few years ago in a car crash.'

'But the man I saw really looked like him,' I told my grandmother, totally unconvinced by what she was saying.

'Well, whoever that man was, he wasn't your father, because your father is dead,' my nanny announced firmly.

At this point, Dr Sweeney broke into my thoughts. 'What was that like for you, being told that your father was dead?'

'I remember feeling very sad. But to be honest, I got over it very quickly. I never had a relationship with my da anyway, so I didn't know what I was missing. I just got on with things, as children do.'

| FALLING APART

When I told Dr Sweeney that I had got over my father's 'death', it was only partly true. In reality, I was so traumatised by my mother leaving that I couldn't take it in, and so, like much else in my life at this time, I buried it somewhere deep down, where I thought it couldn't hurt me. I knew that my nanny was telling me a lie about my father, but I hadn't the heart to care any more.

I had opened my heart to Dr Sweeney because my life depended on it. I knew that to stand any chance of real recovery, I had to tell him the truth, but more importantly to tell myself the truth, about my life. And so I began to keep a journal, to jot down memories of my life as they came to me. I decided that no matter how painful these memories were, I would write them down, as it really helped me to make sense of them and to understand how my trying to bury them had nearly destroyed me. The most painful of these memories were those about my mother and my life after she left. I felt empty inside and, although I couldn't articulate it, I was filled with a rage that at times threatened to overwhelm me.

I was eleven years old and, on the outside, I was still the golden-haired girl who loved school and everything about it. Art and music were my favourite subjects. I used to do a lot of the paintings for our local church and on Saturdays I would go to school for piano lessons with my music teacher. But inside I was really struggling to contain my anger and the constant, nagging feeling that I was worth nothing. I was a time-bomb waiting to go off, and as I grew into adolescence all of the ingredients to light the fuse were beginning to come together.

With the adults in my life in and out of the house, there wasn't always someone at home to keep an eye on me. My grandmother made sure I got up every morning for school and would often see me to the bus stop. She would always ensure that there was a hot meal for me when I came in from school, but because she worked she wasn't always there. I spent most of my time out of the house, hanging around with my friends on the road, playing games with my friend Mary and her older sister and some other kids from the area. My auntie Jacqueline, who lived at home, would call me in at night or to take my asthma medication.

Then I met Katie, a new girl who had moved into a house just two doors away. We quickly became best friends and her family became my own. Her mother and father—Breeda and James—and her five brothers and sisters had all moved into a three-bedroomed house in Ballymun with Breeda's mother, Bernadette. After converting the bathroom into a bedroom, they somehow managed to fit themselves into their house. They had very little financially, but they were closely knit together and seemed very happy as a family. I was very attracted to their closeness and I began to spend most of my time there. Their house was always noisy and full of kids.

I loved spending the night at the O'Connors'. Breeda would wake us up for school and we would all sit around the table together for breakfast: this was new to me. Then the kids would kill each other over who got to use the bathroom first. Breeda would make a chore list for the week, and God forbid that you didn't abide by it. She would ground the kids for weeks, making them do all the housework. I always wanted to be grounded like Katie, but my nanny wasn't strict with me—she didn't need to be because I had always been such a good child.

Every Saturday myself and Katie would be sent to do the

weekly shopping, giving us a sense of responsibility. We thought that we were great, with our shopping list and trolley. One Saturday, on our way back from the shopping centre, we bumped into Katie's sister Susan. She was hanging around the towers in Sillogue. I remember her all done up, as if she was going somewhere. Then I realised why. She was with these two young fellas. They were a year or two older than myself and Katie and couldn't have been more than twelve years old. Their names were Steo and Snarts and it turned out that Snarts was Susan's new boyfriend.

I had never met anyone who lived in the blocks before and they looked like little gurriers. Steo was pocket-sized, with sallow skin and a pretty face. Snarts wasn't much taller and looked like the Milky Way kid, with white hair and a dimple in his chin. Myself and Katie weren't impressed with Susan's new friends, but as time went on Susan began to invite them to her house and my whole world began to change.

When the O'Connors moved into our street, kids came out of the woodwork from all over Ballymun. A friendly and open person, Mrs O'Connor opened her doors to all of her children's friends. Nearly every weekend we would have a hop or a dance-off, where all the kids from the area would come to Katie's house for a disco, or we would have a dancing competition. A new world was opening up to me and at first I wasn't sure if I liked it. I was painfully shy and I didn't know how to act around our new friends.

Steo and Snarts listened to techno music that I had never even heard of before. They would arrive at Katie's, smoking cigarettes and wearing baggy jeans, lumber jackets and Paddy caps. All the kids would gather in the sitting-room, where we would blast the stereo and become more hyper by the minute. I would usually bury myself in a corner of the sofa, dreading that Katie might ask me to show the other kids the dance we had practised earlier or to sing a song that we had made up ourselves. When she did ask me to dance, I would go red in the face and she would say, 'Don't be going scarlet. C'mon'. I would reluctantly get up and dance, hating every minute of it and wanting the ground to open up and swallow me. Especially the first time Steo asked me to dance with him to a slow set. I'll never forget it. I was tall for my age and towered over him and I felt so silly. He gently put his hands around my waist and I put my hands around his neck. We were barely touching each other. I remember catching Katie's eye a few times and she was grinning from ear to ear. She knew that I liked Steo. 'It's 'orrible being in love when you're 8½. I've got your picture on my wall, I've got your name up on my scarf, Oh it's 'orrible being in love when you're 8½,' played on the stereo, as myself and Steo awkwardly swayed from side to side, doing our best not to stand on each other's toes.

In the beginning I would get really embarrassed around Steo and Snarts, but as time went on I began to feel more comfortable with them. The novelty of going out with Snarts wore off Susan quick enough, so she started seeing Steo's brother, David. David was the same age as Susan, eleven, and looked nothing like his brother. He was a lot taller, with sandy coloured, tousled hair and he took the role of group comedian. We were becoming like a little gang and it was getting bigger by the day. A new girl moved in between Katie and Mary. Her name was Emer. She was a placid girl, the same age as myself. She was skinny with pale skin and had a big mop of dark coffee-coloured curls on her head. Her parents were young and stylish and had two younger kids. Myself and the three girls, Katie, Mary and Emer, became as thick as thieves and never went anywhere without one another.

My grandmother wasn't like the other girls' mothers. Even though she wasn't very strict, it took her a while to come around to the idea of bringing my friends into the house and I would usually have to sneak them in, depending on John's humour. But my grandmother became very fond of my three friends, and when John wasn't there she would let us raid her presses for loads of munchies. My grandmother must have thought that there was going to be a war, because she bought all her groceries in bulk, making sure that I never wanted for anything. For this reason alone, my friends loved coming to my house.

With my grandmother working in Dublin Airport she was making her own money and she wasn't as reliant as before on John, something which pleased her greatly. 'I'm telling ye, Rachael, never rely on a man. Get out there and stand on your own two feet,' she would say to me over and over again. But at the same time as my relationship with my nanny became closer, my relationship with my mother was becoming more and more distant. Although she still visited at the weekend, she had moved into a new flat in Mercer Street with Philip and his father, Mick, my mother's new partner, who was a soldier in the Irish Army at the time. Mick was a stranger to me then. I can only remember meeting him once before they moved into the flat together, at my auntie Marion's wedding to Declan.

However, once she was installed in her new flat, I think my mother made an effort to involve me more in their lives, because she began to invite me over to the flat to mind Philip. My brother was only five at the time. He was tall for his age, with chocolate hair and eyelashes that went on for ever. He was adorable, but he was a real handful, always doing the opposite to what my ma told him to do. The flat had only one bedroom, with a separate kitchen and sitting-room, but my mother made it as homely as she could.

My mother had a history of difficult men. Her relationship with my grandfather had never really recovered from her teenage pregnancy, although they had reached an uneasy truce, and my father's relationship with her had been fraught with violence and stress. Unfortunately, it looked as if history might repeat itself with Mick. One night when I was visiting, my ma and Mick came back from the pub. I was lying on the chair in the sitting-room, pretending to be asleep. My ma came straight in and kissed me on the forehead, then she went back into the kitchen with Mick, leaving a whiff of alcohol and perfume behind her. I lay in the dark, trying to hear what they were saying. They were at loggerheads over something. They argued for a few minutes, then everything went calm. I knew that she was ok. They both quietly went to bed, as I glided off into a deep sleep.

Mick and my mother subsequently had an argument that left her very upset. I don't know the details but he left the flat in a hurry. As soon as Mick was gone I ran in to my mother. She sat up straight in the bed and reached out her arms to me. She was crying. She held me in her arms, saying that she was so sorry. I became hysterical. She took me by the hand and brought me out to the sitting-room where she sat me down and knelt before me.

'Rachael, make a promise to me?' she asked.

I couldn't look at her. 'What?' I said, still hyperventilating.

'Promise me that you'll finish school and go to college.'

I didn't know what she was talking about. 'Why? Where are you going?' I asked. For a moment I thought that she was going to die and that was her last wish.

'Nowhere; just promise, will you?'

'Ok, I promise.' At the time I didn't know what she was talking about, but now I do. She wanted me to have a better start in life than she had, so that I would be able to make better choices. She wanted me to have an education, so that I could grab the opportunities that she had missed and not end up like her, depending on an unpredictable man to get by in life. I wish I had understood her better then.

'And will you not say anything to nanny about this?'

I looked at her red-rimmed eyes. 'Ok, I won't.' I never did tell my grandmother. I kept my mouth shut for a long time about that row and about others, but the more I kept to myself, the more lost I became. The hurt and fear were simply too much for me to handle, so I buried them. But the strain was beginning to show. My grades in school were beginning to drop. I was losing interest. In spite of my mother's plea to me, I couldn't see the value of getting an education, not when hanging around the tower blocks was becoming more appealing. Going home to do my homework just wasn't an option for me. After all, what was the point, I thought, when I had nobody to answer to, nobody who would take a real interest in me? I guess my family just assumed that I was ok. But it wasn't long until they found out the truth.

———

It all happened very quickly, now that I look back on it. I was only eleven, and when I think about this time of my life it just seems like a blur. I remember the first time I smoked a cigarette. All my friends were smoking and I needed to prove to them that I was part of the gang and up for a laugh. The only thing was, I was afraid of smoking in front of Steo and Snarts. I was convinced that I would do it wrong and make a holy show of myself. I thought that they would laugh at me. So I practised smoking until I knew I looked cool enough to stand there with them and take a puff.

The days rolled into one-another and before I knew it I was drinking alcohol and smoking hash as well. School quickly became a hindrance, so myself and Katie started to go on the mitch, spending every minute we had in Sillogue. We would bring a spare set of clothes with us and get changed in the tower blocks. Then we would wait for Steo and Snarts to fall out of bed. We could always depend on them to have a bit of hash. We would usually sit in the sun, slag everyone off and get stoned out of our heads. I began to wonder why people even went to school or work, when they could easily draw the dole, sit on their arses and get stoned all day, like we did.

I was having the time of my life and I never wanted it to end. Especially when Steo asked me to go off with him. We had become the best of friends and I was so impressed with how cool and laid-back he was, saying all the right things at just the right time, making everyone in awe of him. But I was the one that he wanted to be with. I felt special. My confidence was sky-high. I was no longer this shy and reserved little girl who shrank when someone looked at her. Especially when I smoked hash. I was the life and soul of the party, willing to do anything for a laugh.

I now had a boyfriend, my body was going through so many changes and I was beginning to wonder about sex. All my friends were talking about it and I would play along, pretending that I knew what they were talking about. But I was completely in the dark.

'Did Steo try anything on you?' Katie would ask me when we were alone.

I got embarrassed at the thought of it. 'No. Why? Did Snarts try anything on you?'

'I wouldn't fuckin' let him if he tried.'

Myself and Steo were spending more and more time together. We would lie on his bed and I would tell him all about my family. He would hold me in his arms and make me feel like the most important person in the world. We had been together for two years before he tried anything at all.

———

One day, I lay on my bed staring into space, smoking a joint and listening to Cat Stevens' 'Wild World'. The words of the song, 'I'll always remember you as a child, girl,' made me feel empty inside, as though I were missing something. For some reason I thought about my father. I vaguely remembered him holding me on his lap, singing and playing with me. I thought about my christening photograph. Him with his hand gently touching my head. Thoughts of the man in Finglas, who had called my name and who looked just like my da, surfaced. Was my da really dead? I thought. Have they being lying to me all these years? I felt butterflies in my stomach and a flicker of hope being born. I wondered what he'd look like now. Whether he had more kids or not. Would he recognise me if he saw me on the street? Would he hold me tightly in his arms, like any dad would, promising to protect me from this wild world? There and then, I made the decision to find out the truth about whether he was alive or dead, once and for all.

Chapter 4

I'LL ALWAYS REMEMBER YOU

'Only one more flight of stairs to go,' I said to Katie as I struggled to catch my breath and dragged myself up to the top floor of the tower block. We had run all the way from my grandmother's house up to the eighth storey of the flats after we'd stolen bottles of Black Russian vodka from my uncle Laurence. Just as I was about to take the cap off our prize possession I heard a door open and close. 'Hide it, hide it,' Katie urged as I shoved the bottle into my jacket. I held my breath as I heard footsteps coming towards us.

'Alright, girls?' said this rough-looking lad with a heavy Dublin accent. He looked down at my jacket. 'Wha have yiz got there? Don't tell me yiz are drinking, are ye? Ah, don't worry, love, I won't tell your da,' he said, grinning and looking me straight in the eye.

'Why, do you know me da?' I asked, puzzled by his comment.

'Ah, yeah. You're Con Geraghty's daughter, aren't ye?'

'How d'you know that?' I asked, hanging on his every word.

'I know your da and his bird, Marion Carey, fuckin' years.'

'Would you be able to tell me where he lives?' I tried, feeling like my heart would burst through my chest at any given moment.

'Give us a sup of your drink and I'll tell ye,' he smiled.

I glanced at Katie who sat motionless beside me and then handed over our bottle of vodka. I watched his every movement as he opened the bottle and slowly took a swig from it. Then suddenly he made a dash down the stairs, taking two and three steps at a time, and after peeling my jaw off the floor I chased after him. But it was too late. He was gone.

I stood alone, looking up and down the desolate street, as the reality of my father being alive sank in. 'Where's that other bottle of vodka?' was all I could say to my friend when she finally caught up with me.

'Oh my God, did you hear what he said about your da? And the gobshite robbed our drink,' she said, gasping for air.

My head was spinning and I couldn't think straight.

————

It was a night for getting in out of the cold and getting drunk. I could feel the warmth of the fire as I entered our new hideout, a basement shed under the eight-storey block. The sound of UB40 came from the stereo, while Steo and Snarts and some other friends sat on crates, skinning up spliffs and laughing amongst themselves. Steo's face looked soft by the light of the fire. He looked at me and smiled as I snuggled into him for comfort. Before I knew it I had forgotten all about my da. I could no longer understand what people were saying. Everything was becoming a blur. But it didn't matter—I was with Steo and no-one could hurt me.

————

I felt paralysed. I could hear Steo crying, people shouting and dogs barking. My clothes were wet and somebody was dragging me from one place to another. My mind was racing, but I couldn't move my body. I felt a burning slap to my face. 'Wake up, Rachael!' I opened my eyes and realised that I had blacked out. I was lying on the floor of the shed with my top up around my neck and the shed was flooded.

'I thought you were dead,' I heard Steo say as I tried to focus on my surroundings. But all I could do was vomit. Everything became a blur again until I felt a tube being forced down my neck and into my stomach.

I finally came to my senses, but I had no idea where I was. And then the memories of the night before came rushing back to me as I stared at the bunnies painted on the wall in Temple Street Hospital. I remembered that I had drunk a bottle of vodka and smoked some hash, and the rest is a blank. Then I saw my mother. She was sitting beside my bed, pale and stoney-faced. I wished I hadn't woken up. I closed my eyes, telling myself, 'Never again.' Perhaps it was just finding out about my da that had set me off, I rationalised.

But in fact, 'never again' was just the beginning. I was twelve years old and quickly becoming more and more disconnected from my family. Hanging around freezing cold tower blocks and mitching from school was becoming the norm for me. Nobody seemed to care about what we got up to, either our families or anyone else. We could light our bonfires and drink our illegally purchased flagons of Scrumpy Jack without anyone blinking an eye. Every so often we would get a visit from the gardaí: '5.0 5.0,' somebody would shout, warning us of their approach, giving us barely enough time to stash our hash and our alcohol.

On one occasion the 'blue bottles' snuck into the block and caught us red-handed with our joints and lumps of hash. Before I knew it I was being marshalled away from my friends, out to the front of the block. It was broad daylight and all I could think of was, what if somebody saw me standing here with this guard? They would definitely think I was a rat.

'Well, what's your name?' asked the garda.

'Rachael Keogh,' I replied, anxiously looking around me, hoping that no-one was watching.

'What are you doing hanging around here? And why aren't you in school? You're going to end up in trouble if you keep hanging around here, d'you realise that?'

I didn't respond. I had been well trained never, under any circumstances, to talk to the gardaí. 'Tell them nothing,' I was warned by my friends. 'They're only scum.' So I just nodded my head at the garda, shuffling childishly from side to side, feeling like an ant in comparison to this man who was built like a tank.

'I have a daughter and she looks just like you,' the garda continued. 'Now, if I catch you around here again you're in trouble, ok? So go on. Go home,' he demanded.

But I didn't go home. I hid in another block until they were gone and off I went back up to my friends, completely unfazed by what had happened. I desperately wanted my friends to like me and I was willing to go to great lengths for their approval.

My need to be liked and accepted became my motive for everything I did. So much so that I began to steal from my grandmother in order to buy hash for myself and my friends. I kept this a secret from everyone, knowing well that what I was doing was wrong. But it was worth it when my friends patted me on the back, saying, 'Nice one, Rach, fair play to ya.' I was definitely part of the gang then. My friends needed me. They could depend on me to do anything. I was intelligent and clever, but I was quickly becoming devious in my ways, telling nobody anything and holding my cards close to my chest where my family was concerned.

I was getting bored with Sillogue, so myself and Katie began to hang around with two girls we went to school with. They seemed up for a laugh and when they told me that they sniffed air-freshener and got a great buzz off it, I was really curious. Within a few hours I had a bottle of Glade in my hand, sitting in my grandmother's kitchen. 'Just put the bottle in a plastic bag, put it up to your mouth, spray and inhale,' the girls said.

I was afraid. But I couldn't let the girls know this. So without saying anything I went into the toilet and did as I was told. All it took was one blast. The air-freshener rapidly worked its way into my mouth, down into my lungs and up into my brain. 'Ha ha ha, are ye alright in there, love?' I could hear someone say outside the toilet. I felt fuzzy inside and the room began to spin. Reality was becoming dreamy, and before I knew it I was hallucinating. My hands were bound together with twine. My whole body was being controlled by what seemed to be a black cat. He wore a luminous yellow bandana and he spoke to me in a computerised voice. 'Getting down to the limit. Getting down to the limit,' he said, as he pulled on the twine, dragging my body down to the floor. He then put glue on my ear and stuck my head to the toilet bowl and there I stayed for I don't know how long.

'What the hell is going on?' The toilet door swung open and there stood my grandmother. 'What are you doing?' she screamed, a look of disbelief on her face.

I still felt as though I were dreaming. 'I'm stuck. I'm not able to move,' I told her. 'What do you mean, you're stuck? Get up off the floor,' she screeched and stormed off into the kitchen. 'Come on, get out,' I heard her say to the two girls. The fear of facing my grandmother gave me the ability to peel myself from the toilet bowl and without saying a word to her I ran out the front door.

The rest of the day became a haze. After sniffing more air-freshener, we decided to take a walk into the city centre. I was struggling to keep up with the girls and I kept drifting in and out of reality. Before I knew what was happening, my friends had disappeared. It was the middle of the night and I had no idea where I was. I was beginning to panic, but I had completely lost control over myself. Once again, I blacked out. Eventually I woke up, but somebody was carrying me. It was a man who wore a white coat. He lay me down on the pavement and vanished. It was morning time and suddenly my friends were there. 'Where did you go? We were looking for you everywhere.' 'I don't know where I was. You just left me on my own,' I spat. I stood up and realised that my hands were black with the dirt and the front of my shirt was ripped. I felt like I had been living in a nightmare. I was just relieved that it was over. But I knew that I had another nightmare to face when I got home.

I was getting into more and more trouble at home as my behaviour began to spiral out of control. Either I would be drunk, high on air-freshener or hash, or stealing from my grandmother. I became increasingly aggressive and stroppy and I took most of my aggression out on John, whom I adored. One day, when I had just started using drugs, John lost his temper. It was dinner time and when I arrived up the garden path, stoned, he smashed a plate of food in my face, disgusted at the state of me. I was so enraged that I fought back and managed to shove him through the front window. There he lay on the front lawn, hair covered in curly kale.

It seems almost comical now, but it wasn't then, as my family became increasingly worried about my behaviour and unsure what to do about it. My grandmother had a lot on her plate: John, her children, her job and me and, although she was aware of what I was up to, perhaps it was easier for her to think it was 'just a phase' than to acknowledge that it might be something more serious. Fighting turned to stealing, first just small stuff here and there, but eventually anything that wasn't nailed down. And I became a seasoned liar, making up stories to get my family's attention. Once I pretended the house had been broken into, and I called my auntie Jacqueline when my family were having a meal in my auntie Marion's house, begging her to come back home. Looking back, I was crying out for some attention from my family, some recognition of the fact that I existed. I would ultimately get all the attention I wanted, in all the wrong ways.

———

Joanne was a quiet young girl who lived in the same area as me. She had milky-blonde hair, with pale skin. She always seemed to be on her own. So, when I saw her hanging around Sillogue with my other friends I was quite surprised. She seemed really funny and down-to-earth and we got on with each other straight away.

She told myself and Katie that she had a boyfriend from Poppintree. 'He's a bit older and he goes to all the raves,' she said. Myself and Katie were intrigued. Raves were new to us. 'There's a rave on this weekend called The Pavilion,' she continued. 'If you want, you can come with me. I'll introduce ye to me fella and his mates,' she said, with a glint in her eye.

Myself and Katie could barely contain ourselves. We were so excited about going to The Pavilion. Everyone seemed to be going to these raves and I was eager to find out what all the fuss was about. After drinking a couple of cans and smoking a few joints, we made our way to meet Joanne. It was a warm night and the orange lights on the streets guided us up to Poppintree.

'Where is this place?' I asked, not knowing where I was going.

'As far as I know it's in the back fields,' Joanne replied, as much in the dark as I was. After making our way through some bushes, I realised we were in an open field. It was pitch black and I couldn't see a thing. I could hear dance music coming from the mid-distance. We followed its trail, with our hands held out in front of us, hoping that we wouldn't fall in the dark.

'Is this it?' Katie said, disappointed, as we arrived at what seemed to be a concrete changing room for football players. I held onto Katie's hand as we followed Joanne inside. It was like nothing I had ever seen before. I was used to going to innocent little parties where all the girls would sit together, giggling amongst themselves, waiting for one of the boys to ask them up for a slow set. This was in a league of its own. One that was much more dangerous. There was nobody on the door asking me for ID. There was no fancy bar, and there were no disco balls hanging from the ceiling at this club.

The first thing that hit me was the body heat and the overwhelming smell of sweat. For such a small place, a lot of people fitted inside. The place was packed with kids just like me. All the boys had their tops off and everyone seemed to be in a trance, dancing exactly the same way, like puppets on a string. I was afraid and excited, all at the same time.

'Up this way, keep going to the back,' Joanne urged, as myself and Katie looked on in amazement. We pushed and shoved our way up to the back, which was badly lit by a couple of candles. 'Redser, these are me mates, Katie and Rachael,' Joanne shouted, trying to introduce us to her boyfriend. Redser had no interest in myself and my friend. He had a deranged look on his face, as if he were possessed. The DJ was in the corner with one hand on his ear-phones and the other on his decks. He was playing music that I had never heard before. They called it 'House Music'.

As my eyes began to adjust to the dark, I noticed that there were people sitting on the ground. They were hunched over, inhaling something that they were burning on tin-foil. It appeared to be hash oil, but I wasn't sure. Joanne made her way over to one of them. She tipped him on the shoulder and he glanced up. 'Tony, this is Katie and Rachael,' she said again. 'Alright,' he said with a cylinder of tin-foil hanging from his mouth. 'Are yiz looking for any Es?'

'What's Es?' I asked.

Tony burst out laughing, smoke coming out of his mouth. 'Yeah, right, as if yiz don't know what Es are. D'ye want them or not?' There was a pause. Then Tony realised that we weren't joking. 'Wha'—have yiz never done Es before?'

We shook our heads.

'Ah, yiz don't know what yiz are missing. They're fuckin' deadly. If yiz want, I can get ye Mad Bastards, White Doves or Mitsubishis. You're probably better off going with the White Doves if it's your first time, and only take a half of one.'

'Is everyone on Es here?' I asked Joanne.

She looked around the room at the crush of bodies, all dancing as if in a trance. 'Yeah, I think so.'

'What will we do?' I said to Katie, unsure if I wanted to try out this new drug. With hash, I knew where I was, but this was different. 'D'ye wanna get some?' Like me, Katie didn't seem too sure, but she said yes anyway. We paid Tony ten pounds each and swallowed half an E each. We were completely unaware of what we were putting into our bodies. But everyone seemed to be having so much fun we didn't think much of it.

'There's nothing happening, Joanne. How long does it take for these to work?' I asked about twenty minutes later.

'You should be feeling it by now,' she said, looking as if the drug had taken hold.

'Well, I'm not,' I replied. 'Will I take the other half?'

'If ye want,' she said, shrugging. So I took the other half and within minutes I began to feel really alert. My senses were heightened. The music was louder. My thinking was clearer. Even my body felt lighter. A lovely warm sensation was dancing its way from my toes up into my head, massaging every cell in my body and washing away all my teenage stresses. The intensity of it overwhelmed me, making it difficult for me to breathe. I was losing my balance and my eyes began to roll into the back of my head. But I had never felt this good in my whole life.

'Katie, I'm fuckin' out of it,' I whispered to my friend, as if it were some sort of secret.

'So am I,' she said, looking around the rave as if she thought her mother was watching.

'Are you alright?' I asked her, feeling genuinely concerned. 'C'mere, give us a hug.' We embraced each other for what seemed like an eternity. Once again, I felt a rush of energy surge through my body, making myself and my best friend spin. The rave had become busier. It was at its peak and everyone was on the same wavelength. All that we wanted to do was dance.

———

'It takes five seconds
Five seconds of decision

Five seconds to realise your purpose here on the planet
It takes five seconds to realise that it's time to move
It's time to get down with it
Brothers, it's time to testify and I want to know
Are you ready to testify...'

———

The music penetrated my soul.

'It's coming, it's coming,' people were shouting, with their hands in the air and everyone exploded into dance. We danced until the early hours of the morning, unable to stop, high on the music.

When The Pavilion was almost empty, myself and my two friends decided to go home. 'Jaysus, you would want a fuckin' boat to get across to that place. Look at me, I'm full of muck,' Katie said, as myself and Joanne laughed.

'But it was deadly, wasn't it?' she said.

'Yeah, it really was,' I replied, still floating.

'Ah, you're deadly swell,' she said.

'So are you, and you are swell, Joanne,' I told them.

'I just can't get over it. It was deadly, wasn't it?' Katie said again. And this is how it was, all the way home.

Soon The Pavilion became the highlight of my week. On the rare occasions that I went to school, I would sit in class fantasising about the weekend ahead. The rest of the time we would hang around the blocks, talking animatedly about different things that had happened in The Pavilion, feeling euphoric and re-living the weekend just gone.

My family were beginning to notice a change in my behaviour. I was sullen and indifferent at home and I had no interest in anything that they had to say to me. They didn't understand me anyway, I told myself. They could never understand what my life was like now, mitching from school, staying out all day and all night without telling them a thing. I began to lie compulsively about everything, even to my friends. My appetite had disappeared and I was living on packets of crisps and chocolate. My nanny began to notice different things going missing from the house. I needed money to buy my drugs, which I was now taking every day and so I had begun to steal from them: jewellery, clothes, anything that I thought I could sell easily to buy drugs. My grandmother confronted my friends about the missing clothes and jewellery.

My friends, who were still only taking the odd E tablet at the weekends, or smoking hash, became worried about my increasing dependence. 'D'ye see those junkies over there, Rachael,' my boyfriend Steo said, one day, pointing to the drug addicts hanging around the shops. 'If you keep going the way you're going, you'll end up like them.'

This was the funniest thing I had ever heard. 'Me?' I said in a high-pitched voice. 'Look who's talking! You're the one that will end up like that. You'll be hanging around, strung out to bits. But don't worry, I'll give ye a wave when I'm driving past in my Porsche,' I told him arrogantly. I waited for him to laugh. But Steo didn't find it funny.

Myself and Steo broke up not long afterwards. I had lost interest in him and everyone else in Sillogue and in the tower blocks. They were so immature, I thought to myself. They just never wanted to do anything but doss around the blocks all day, talking about the same things, day in, day out. I had other things on my mind. My new friends, Joanne and the others in Poppintree, seemed to fit better with the new me. At least they didn't get on my case about taking drugs. And we were always guaranteed a bit of excitement.

My quest to find out more about my father continued. One day, myself and Katie anxiously knocked on Marion Carey's door. I had asked a couple of old-time junkies if they knew where she lived. I was almost certain that if anyone knew where my father was, she would be the person to tell me.

'She's not here, Katie. C'mon, let's go,' I said now, but just as we were about to walk away the door opened. I recognised the woman's face. For a second she looked confused, then she smiled. 'Ah, Rachael, me little princess. I knew you'd come knocking on my door. C'mon inside. Who's this with you? Is this your little friend?'

'Yeah, this is my friend Katie,' I said shyly.

'Ah, nice to meet you, love,' she drawled. And before I knew it, she was leading us up her long dark hallway and into her kitchen. It looked just like the flat that I had lived in with my mother and father when I was a toddler. 'I think I know why you're here, love. You're looking for your daddy, aren't you?'

'Yeah, someone told me that you knew him,' I replied.

'Well, you've come to the right place. Your daddy has been waiting all these years for you to come and find him. Do you want a cup of tea? Go on into the sitting-room and make yourselves at home. I'll be in in a minute and I'll tell yous all about it.'

'This isn't happening,' I whispered to Katie as we sat down on Marion's shabby brown couch. I looked around the softly lit room, taking in pictures of her three little boys. I wondered if they were my half-brothers.

'Now, loves, there yous go,' Marion said, placing the cups in front of myself and Katie. 'Now, tell me,' she asked me, 'how long have you been looking for your da?'

I told Marion everything, about my mother leaving and about my father calling to me that day from across the street. 'Ah, Jaysus,' she said, putting her arm around me. 'Well, your da will be over the moon. He missed you so much and he's always talking about ye.'

I could barely take in what she was saying. Even the word 'da' was alien to me. I didn't have a da.

'To be honest with you, chicken,' she continued, 'me and your da are partners. We've been together now for years. These are my sons Kevin and David,' she said, showing me the photos. But she said nothing about the other boy. 'This is my mother's flat. Myself and your da live in Coultry. So, what I'll do is, I'll tell your da to meet you somewhere if you like,' she smiled at me expectantly.

I felt anxious. Everything was happening way too fast. But I acted cool and played along. 'Yeah, ok,' I said, hearing my voice shake.

'I'll tell you what,' she continued. 'Why don't you meet your da on Tuesday at five o'clock outside the Kingfisher restaurant in town. I'll make sure he's there, ok?'

Unable to summon the courage to say anything, I just nodded and we left. My heart was in my mouth.

I didn't know what to make of meeting my father. Although I had barely thought of him over all the years, the prospect of meeting him now, after everything that had happened with my mother, seemed overwhelming to me. What if I didn't like him, I thought, or if he wasn't how I imagined him to be? What was the man who used to attack my mother really like? Was he a changed man, or still the same? The whole week was tortuous. Every day dragged on and I thought Tuesday wouldn't come quick enough. My friends in Sillogue were shocked to hear about my da and they were concerned about me meeting him after all this time. So we made a plan that, once I'd met him, they would follow me and him around town and watch his every move. For all we knew he could have been an axe murderer.

Finally, it was Tuesday. My big day and no matter how many joints I smoked, I couldn't get rid of the anxiety gnawing at my stomach. I was on the hop from school, walking around Ballymun in my uniform, as though I were invisible. I decided to take a stroll through the shopping centre. The usual riff-raff were there, junkies doing their deals and looking like death warmed up.

Then I saw Marion Carey standing amongst them. Ah no, just keep walking, I thought to myself, almost breaking into a sprint. Then I heard her voice, calling me. 'Rachael,' she shouted, loud enough for the whole shopping centre to hear her. I had no choice but to turn around.

Then I saw him. I knew it was him straight away. My father. He was standing there with all the junkies. My heart sank.

'C'mere, love, for a minute,' Marion said, waving me over. I was dizzy and felt weak at the knees. 'This is your daddy, Rachael.' She motioned towards the man standing beside her.

I looked at his worn-out face. Years of using drugs had obviously taken their toll. His brown hair was long and greasy and his shiny black bomber jacket was like something from the eighties. I immediately knew that I hadn't got my fashion sense from him. He was gazing at me lovingly. He came to me and held me in his arms. He smelt of old musk. When he pulled away I could tell that he was crying. 'I can't believe how grown up you've got,' he said with pride, as he ushered me away from his friends. 'You look just like your mother. How is she anyway?' he asked.

'She's ok,' I said, trying to hide my fear.

'She doesn't know that you're meeting me, does she?'

'No. They all told me that you were dead.'

He shook his head and smiled, as though he wasn't one bit surprised. 'Rachael, I need to tell you something, before anyone else does. You've probably already guessed. I'm a drug addict.'

Although this was perfectly obvious, part of me was disappointed, but the other part thought, this is cool. I have a young da who takes drugs. Deadly. 'Yeah, I kinda knew by the people that you're hanging around with,' I told him, eyeing his friends. 'I sometimes take drugs as well,' I told him, like he was my new best friend and I was trying to impress him.

He laughed, 'You're joking,' he said.

'No, I'm serious, I smoke hash and sometimes I take acid,' I brazenly told him.

'Who's giving you the drugs?' he asked.

'Ah, just people around the area.'

'Ok, we'll talk more about it later.'

He'd better not start giving me lectures about drugs, I thought. That'd be rich, coming from him. 'Yeah, I'll see you at five,' I said, and walked off into the shopping centre, unable to believe whether the encounter I'd had was real.

———

At five o'clock that evening, I waited outside the Kingfisher restaurant for my father. My friends stood patiently across the road—after I had met my father earlier in the day, I had run all the way back to Sillogue to tell them all the gossip. We were now on an adventure and my friends were my bodyguards, keeping me safe from my junkie da.

He arrived half an hour late and my friends were getting bored. We decided to go for something to eat—father and daughter, our first meal together. I was already freaked out after our meeting earlier that day and when we got to the restaurant my father sat down beside me, way too close for comfort. I noticed people looking at us. Everyone thinks that I'm his girlfriend, I thought in horror. Then he put his arm around my shoulder. Eww, get your arm off me, I thought, cringing in my own skin. After all my daydreaming about my father, I began to wonder who this stranger sitting beside me was. Was this what *real* fathers and daughters did together? I had no idea. But I knew that it felt horrible.

My friends were nowhere to be seen and I was beginning to panic. I could see my da's lips moving. He was saying something about my ma getting a barring order against him. He had wanted to contact me, but my family wouldn't let him see me. I couldn't take in what he was saying: Get me out of here, get me out of here, I was screaming in my head. My da wasn't doing anything wrong —he was just trying to be a father as he saw it. But I couldn't bear it. It just didn't feel right. I couldn't get away from him quick enough. And when I did, I felt really let down. He wasn't what I had hoped for. I just wanted to cry and I was embarrassed to say that this man was my father.

————

By now I was lost. Lost in my own world of glass and it was about to shatter even more. The questions went round and round in my head: How could my mother do this? How could she not tell me about my father? Why did she keep it a secret? I loved her so much and wanted nothing more than to be like her and be loved by her. But she had lied to me.

I was so angry with my whole family. But it was a silent and muted anger, one that was poisonous and slowly beginning to fester inside me. I wanted nothing to do with my family any more. They had all lied to me. And my mother didn't care anyway. She would dutifully call every Saturday, but although she was there physically, emotionally she seemed detached. No matter what I did, it just wasn't enough to get her attention; it seemed to me that she just didn't want to know. Maybe she doesn't like me because I'm my da's daughter. Maybe she just wants to forget about that part of her life. And that's why she left me with my grandparents, I thought. Well, I'd show her. I wouldn't let her forget about me that quickly.

Chapter 5 ∿

| NO GOING BACK

'We'll get twelve Es—two each for Friday, Saturday and Sunday,' I proposed to Joanne, trying to be organised. We had been given two tickets for a rave in the city centre. Everyone was buzzing about this place and I had started to feel like I was missing out on some serious action.

'Yeah, cool,' Joanne said, as we stood in front of our dealer. Her eyes were wide with excitement. The rave didn't start until around eleven o'clock, so we decided to take an E each and walk into town. It didn't take long for the E to come up on us. We were full of energy and I felt like I could walk all the way to the moon. We chatted to each other the whole time and we got in to town in the blink of an eye, it seemed.

'Sorry, but you're not getting in,' the bouncer said dismissively when we arrived at the club.

'Why not?' we asked indignantly.

'You're just not. You're not old enough for a start and you're not dressed appropriately.' I looked down at my purple Patagonia jacket, my jeans and brand new Air Max trainers. And there was me thinking that I looked great. I didn't understand though. He was letting people in just as young as us and they didn't seem to be dressed appropriately either. What was his problem? I pulled Joanne aside. 'Don't worry, we'll get in. Just wait for a while and we'll ask him again.' I wasn't taking no for an answer. I was getting into the Rave no matter what I had to do. The E had taken full-blown effect, but I was no longer feeling energetic. I wanted to lie down on the ground and go to sleep. I needed to be stimulated to bring me back up. But it needed to be quick.

I noticed people walking around the back way of the club and I wondered if there was another way in. There was. We couldn't believe our luck. Oh my God, I thought. The Pavilion was the Mickey Mouse Club in comparison to this place. I could barely see in front of me. The smoke machine coughed out so much smoke that I didn't know where I was going. But I quickly found my way to the toilet and swallowed another E.

When I glanced in the mirror I realised why the bouncer had turned us away. I looked like a coal-man. My face was black with the dirt, but I had no idea how it had happened. A few minutes later I took another E and then another one. My 'organised' plan for the weekend went up in smoke and before long I had taken Joanne's Es as well, before returning to the dance floor.

'C'mon, get up and don't be scagging,' I heard somebody say, as they shook my shoulder. But I couldn't move. I shook my head and tried to focus on the music: 'Drugs taking their lives, giving them drugs, taking their lives away.' The Empirion track provoked emotions so intense that they had me knocked to the floor. I looked on in awe at everyone dancing. They were like an army of robots. Then I saw Joanne. She was like a banshee. Her hair had turned white, falling all the way down to her ankles. I couldn't take my eyes off her. I watched her in great wonder as she swayed from side to side. Despite the encouragement of others to get up and dance, I stayed on the floor for the whole night.

It wasn't until I got outside into the air that I started to come back to life. 'I can't go home like this, Joanne. My uncle Laurence will know that I took something,' I told her, trying to keep my jaws still. 'I need something to help me come down. I'm fuckin' flying.' I had been told about heroin and how good it was at helping people to come down. 'Will we see if we can get a bit of that stuff off Tony? I heard it brings you down nicely,' I said to Joanne. Tony was one of the dealers at The Pavilion.

She didn't need convincing. 'Yeah, let's go to The Pavilion.'

Tony was there, sitting down the back as usual. He was only too happy to give us some heroin and he even agreed to show us how to do it. 'Here, put the tutor in your mouth and suck when you see the smoke coming out,' he ordered. I was apprehensive, knowing already that if I liked it I would probably be doing it every day, along with the other drugs I was taking. But then I told myself, I wouldn't be doing it every day because I was addicted. I would do it just because I wanted to. And I could stop when I wanted to as well. I was way too clever to become addicted like my da: I would never let myself go that far.

It was as though Tony could read my mind. 'Just don't think about it. It's not going to kill ye,' he reassured me, as he began to burn the heroin. The little brown blob of heroin rolled its way down the tin-foil. I carefully followed it with my tutor, feeling the smoke enter my lungs, tasting like burned toffee on the back of my mouth. After doing two or three lines, I could feel it taking hold. It crawled its way through my body, wrapping me up in a warm, cosy blanket and holding me protectively like a mother. Making me feel like a baby again. This was the feeling that I had longed for all my life. I instantly fell in love.

———

My predictions had become a reality. Myself and Joanne started smoking heroin every day. All my friends were doing it now. Gangs of us, up on the thirteenth floor in the Hedges tower in Ballymun, leaving tin-foil traces all over the walls.

My family sensed that my drug-taking had reached a new level and they began to watch me more closely. One day I was on my way to the flats when I sensed that I was being followed. They must think that I was born yesterday, I thought to myself, knowing full well that my mother and auntie Jacqueline were following me. I stopped in my tracks and turned around and waved at them. 'Hello, I can see you,' I shouted across to them, as they tried to hide themselves behind the health centre. I walked over to them. 'What are you following me for?'

'Rachael, we know exactly what you're up to. You're taking heroin, aren't you?' said my mother, her voice trembling.

'No. Who told you that?' I couldn't believe that she had found out.

'It doesn't matter who told us. We know you are,' she replied. 'And you're taking things from the house so you can pay for your drugs. Where are you going now?' she asked.

'Never you mind. I'm just going over to my friend.'

'Who's your friend? Your father, is it?'

My heart was in my mouth. 'How could it be my father when he's dead?' I spat, glaring at her.

'Rachael, we know that you found out about him. You don't understand what type of person he is. We were only trying to protect you,' my mother implored.

'Yeah, well, I don't need you to protect me, I can do that myself. So leave me alone,' I roared. I ran off as fast as I could, away from the two of them. I was in a rage. How dare my mother offer to protect me, now, when it was too late! Where was she when I really needed her? I certainly didn't need her now.

I needed to get a bit of gear. I thought of my da, who was living in the same block. He had split up with Marion after they'd had a big row. He had met another girl. She was a drug-addict as well and they lived next door to each other. Maybe he'd lend me some money. I knocked on the door of the girlfriend's flat. I didn't beat around the bush. 'Any chance of lending me twenty pounds?' I asked him.

'What's it for?

'A bag of gear.'

He laughed. 'No, I haven't got it.'

'Well, then, have you any gear?'

'I have, but I'm not giving it to you.'

My eyes lit up. I knew that I would get around him. 'Why not? I'm going to do it anyway. So at least you know that I won't be getting into any trouble. I won't go out. I'll do it here. Please, I'm really sick. You're hardly going to see me sick, are you?' I looked at him imploringly.

He looked at me sympathetically. 'You can't. I have no tin-foil.'

'Ok then, I'll have a turn-on.' Instead of smoking the drug, I would inject it. I didn't know what I was saying. I was just desperate to get something into me.

'Not a chance. I won't be responsible for giving you your first turn-on.' My da was horrified.

'Look, it's only a matter of time before I do it anyway. If you don't give it to me, I'll have to go shop-lifting or something and I could end up getting arrested. If I don't get arrested, I'm going to have a turn-on anyway. So you might as well just give it to me.' I was using every skill in manipulation that I had.

He eventually agreed. 'Ok, fair enough. I can't believe you've talked me into this. C'mon into my flat and I'll do it for you.'

I watched him intently as he put the heroin on the spoon along with the citric acid. He then lit a flame underneath the spoon until the powder turned to a dark brown, bubbling liquid. As he prepared the turn-on, my head was screaming. 'What are you doing, Rachael?' the voice said. Your da's about to give you a turn-on, one bit of me thought, unable to believe what I was seeing. This isn't what fathers do. This isn't right. But the other part of me kept urging him on: 'Don't think about it. Just do it.' My head wouldn't stop. But I couldn't say no. I had already gone too far.

My da took my arm and wrapped a tourniquet around it. Don't do it, don't do it, I thought, wanting nothing more than for him to do it. He was just about to stick the needle in my arm when suddenly his girlfriend walked in. We were caught in the act and my da's face turned a ghostly white.

'Con Geraghty, what are you fuckin' doing?' the girlfriend

screamed. 'Take that tourniquet off her arm, now. Oh my God. Wha' the hell are you thinking? Sorry, Rachael, you'll have to go.'

I left my da's flat that day feeling worse than ever before. I wanted to run. Run as far away as possible, from my mother and father, from the world and even from myself. But I knew heroin would give me the comfort that I needed. It would never let me down and I could always depend on it to make me feel nothing.

————

I was only thirteen years old. But already the heroin had me in its grip, twisting me from the inside out, taking over my mind, my body and even my soul. I despised myself for the person I was becoming. I couldn't bear to think about what I was doing to my grandmother, robbing from her almost every day to feed my measly drug habit. She couldn't bear to look at my old friends, Katie, Emer and Mary, who were still going to school and doing well for themselves. Even though Katie had taken drugs, once her parents found out they had punished her severely and grounded her for months. My friends reminded my grandmother of how I should have been. She became bitter because they were doing so well and I wasn't. I was falling apart.

My family may have had its difficulties, but they didn't know about drugs and they had never imagined that I would end up like this, high on drugs most of the time, robbing from them when I wasn't, just to get high again. They couldn't see why the blonde bubbly child they had known would turn into this mess. They decided to seek help at the Trinity Court Methadone Programme, but they were assured that I wasn't recognised as a drug addict. They all breathed a sigh of relief for a while—they could ignore the problem, telling themselves that I was going through a phase, one that I would surely grow out of. But the reality was far from this. I was growing into it. Rapidly spiralling head first into addiction and out of control, until they could no longer bury their heads in the sand and pretend it wasn't happening. They decided to take drastic action.

Chapter 6 ∾

| RESCUE PLANS

My legs were agitated and my nose was running. I hadn't got the energy to get out of bed and I wondered if this was 'the sickness' that everyone was talking about, the sickness of withdrawal? I knew my grandfather was downstairs, cooking one of his favourites, sweetbreads or something else which turned my stomach. I could hear him talking to somebody, but I didn't recognise the other person's voice. It seemed to be someone with a Spanish accent, though. He's getting worse by the day, I thought. Letting any Tom, Dick or Harry into the house: John had a habit of meeting complete strangers and inviting them into the house for a cup of tea.

Then I heard the kitchen door open. They were coming up the stairs. I hid under my blankets, pretending to be asleep as my bedroom door opened.

'Rachael, I want you to meet somebody.' It wasn't my grandfather but my mother's boyfriend, Mick. Ever since that row in my mother's flat, I had been suspicious of Mick, but I could see why she stayed with him—he was well off now and offered her a secure, comfortable existence. Also, Mick had taken an interest in me, letting me come out and about with him for the business he now ran and accompanying me to the bus stop to make sure I didn't mitch off school. He was with some man who looked like he was Spanish.

'Hi, really nice to meet you,' said the stranger. 'My name is Donal.'

Donal, me arse, I thought, he was mixed race and spoke with a Spanish accent—he didn't look one bit like a Donal. What was he doing in my room anyway? I was still half asleep and I wasn't impressed with my grandfather letting them come up to me. 'Wow, your bedroom is amazing,' he continued. 'You obviously love Bob Marley,' 'Donal' said, looking around at my huge collection of posters. 'Do you know, I live just next to Jamaica.' A handsome man, well groomed and who appeared to be in his forties, Donal looked like a film star. I was immediately intrigued by him and the fact that he lived beside Jamaica. It was my dream to go there some day.

'I am from a small country called Cuba. Have you ever heard of it?' Donal asked me, solving the mystery of his nationality.

'Oh, yeah,' I replied, not knowing where he was talking about, but wanting to appear intelligent.

'Mick tells me you're having problems with the drugs and you want to get clean,' Donal continued. The penny dropped. It was a set-up. My mother had obviously persuaded Mick to use one of his business contacts to see if he could 'sort me out'—and as far as she was concerned if I could be spirited quietly away in the process, so much the better. At this stage in my relationship with my mother, it was very much out of sight out of mind—if I wasn't there the problem could be ignored. And Mick, who liked me, could be persuaded to intervene.

'Yeah, I do,' I said, lying through my teeth again. I had no intention of giving up drugs. They helped me to forget everything. I was fifteen years old and for the previous two years heroin had been my comfort and my support. I wasn't ready to stop now.

'Well, if you like, you can come and stay with me in Cuba. I am a doctor over there and I could train you in as my secretary. You could even visit Jamaica. It is only a boat ride away. If you don't like it you can always come home.'

Were my ears deceiving me? Was this really happening? I knew that Mick had all kinds of business contacts overseas—and would later learn that Mick had paid Donal to take me—but this 'plan' seemed so bizarre I thought it had to be a joke. 'You don't have to make a decision now. Just think about it and let me know,' Donal continued, as if sensing my disbelief.

I played with the idea of going to Cuba for a couple of days. Fantasising about the boat ride to Jamaica and seeing with my own eyes the very house in which Bob Marley was ambushed and shot. Hanging out with the locals, smoking reefers until sunset. But then I would dismiss the idea. Sure I didn't even know this man, Donal, at least nothing more than that he was a contact of Mick's and owned property in Cuba. How could I possibly survive on my own in a strange country like that? I had never been further than Poppintree in my life. The whole thing was far too bizarre for my liking—and God forbid that I would have to leave Ballymun anyway.

But my family had other plans. Within a couple of months of meeting Donal I found myself on a plane bound for Cuba with the plan that I would be Donal's 'secretary'. My mother and my uncle Laurence accompanied me on my journey. It took us five days to get there: from Ireland to England, England to France, France to Barcelona, Barcelona to the USA, USA to Mexico, Mexico to Venezuela and Venezuela to our final destination, Cuba. It was the longest five days of my life. Being constantly stuck on planes with my mother and Laurence wasn't my idea of having fun. I felt angry, lost and resentful at being sent so far away.

We arrived in Havana and the first thing that hit me was the heat. Even though the sun was going down the air was heavy and sweet. I hadn't once thought of drugs, and for the first time in ages I began to feel excited at the possibility of starting afresh. Maybe this plan might actually work, I thought, even if the whole thing wasn't exactly my idea.

We were greeted at the airport not by Donal but by our tour guides. It was just as well, as the security police didn't seem one bit friendly. They were everywhere, watching everything, dressed in military uniform, looking at us suspiciously, wondering why we were here—in those days, Cuba wasn't yet a holiday destination, so three white faces looked distinctly out of place. I felt jet-lagged and I was relieved to finally get to our hotel and to have a comfortable bed to sleep in. Something wasn't right, though. I could feel it in my bones. My ma and Laurence were acting really strange, leaving their suitcases behind in the taxi and only taking mine out.

Then I noticed the nurses. It wasn't a hotel at all. It was some sort of a hospital. I was quickly ushered to my room. What the hell is going on? I thought to myself as I took in my surroundings. There was an oxygen mask hanging over my bed and a television hanging from the wall. Then my mother and my uncle sat down in front of me. 'I suppose you're wondering what's going on?' said Laurence. I knew exactly what was going on. They had lied to me again. I couldn't look at them.

'Rachael, we didn't know what else to do,' he continued. 'You're completely out of control. We tried bringing you to Trinity Court and that didn't work. What were we supposed to do? This is a detox centre and they will help you to come off the drugs. You only have to stay here for one week and that's it.' They sat there, waiting for me to respond. But I couldn't. My mind was blank and I was no longer in my own body.

'Myself and Laurence will be staying at a hotel just up the road,' my mother assured me. 'If you need anything, just ask the nurse.' She kissed me on the forehead and they were gone.

I couldn't believe that they had left me on my own in this foreign place—I was bewildered, tired and couldn't credit that my mother and Laurence had dumped me here.

The week came and went, as I spent my days watching HBO and feeling numb. The nurses gave me my daily dose of medication and spoke to me in a language that I couldn't understand. My mother and Laurence came to visit, telling me about the fancy hotel that they were staying in and trying to humour me in different ways. 'Rachael, I really can't believe how well you're taking all this,' said my mother as she pottered around my room. But I wasn't taking it well at all. I was gritting my teeth and bearing it, wishing the week away.

'We can't go on like this, you know,' my mother continued. 'We know what you are doing, Rachael,' she said, before rapidly changing the subject. 'Anyway, next week, we are flying to Holguín. We'll stay in a really nice hotel and we'll have a great time,' she reassured me. I couldn't see myself enjoying a holiday after this, but I nodded my head, pretending to share her enthusiasm.

One week later and I was relieved my detox was over. My drug habit wasn't that severe, so with the medication I was given I didn't feel a thing. If nothing else, I had my family off my back and I could look forward to going to Holguín, free from the horrible tension that had lingered between us up until now.

It was as though I had stepped into a time-warp in Holguín. Another world, where time stood still, oblivious to the world outside and to any life beyond its own. A world rich in history, with a mix of Spanish and African culture pulsating through its streets and a mish-mash of colours decorating its old colonial buildings. The Cuban people appeared to be impoverished, but seemed content with their lot, staring at us in wonderment with our blonde hair and fair skin. 'Que linda, Que linda,' the men would mumble as we walked past.

My mother seemed baffled. 'How do they know my name?' she asked Maria, our tour guide.

'Oh no, they don't know your name. They're saying that you're beautiful,' she answered, laughing heartily. Maria stayed with us the whole time, telling us all about Cuba and its roots, about the arrival of African slaves, about Fidel Castro and communism. I would be fascinated now, but then I really had no interest in what she was saying. I hadn't come to Cuba for a guided tour or even for a detox. I had been made to come, lured there by the promise of a job which I knew now didn't exist. But while I was here, the main attraction was the sun. I couldn't wait to find a beach and burn myself to a crisp.

So, I found it odd when we started driving away from the city. Then I saw a sign, which read, EL QUINQUE. 'I hope we're not going to another centre,' I said to my mother, immediately thinking that the sign meant 'clinic'.

'What do you mean? I told you already that we were,' she answered, looking at me as if I were mad.

'No, you didn't. You said that we were staying at a hotel. I can't believe you're doing this. I'm not going to another treatment centre,' I screamed, realising what was going on and becoming more hysterical by the minute.

'Let's just see what it's like, ok?' my mother implored.

'No, I don't care what you say, I'm not going.'

'Ok, if you don't like it, you don't have to stay.' She took me by the hand and led me in through the gates.

'I'm not staying,' I repeated, as we passed a security guard who had a gun attached to his waist. Then we were greeted by the receptionist. '*Hola, como esta?*' he said, smiling.

'Fuck off,' I said under my breath and turned my back to him. Then I was distracted by a commotion just feet away from where I stood. Two men emerged from one of the houses, wheeling a stretcher in front of them. I couldn't believe my eyes when I saw the black plastic body-bag.

'Oh my God,' I heard my ma say behind me, before she covered my eyes with her hands.

'I am really sorry that you had to see that,' said the receptionist, leading us away from the scene.

'What's happened?' Laurence asked him.

'Well, you see, El Quinque has three phases: for the first two phases, patients cannot leave the grounds without supervision. But after therapeutic evaluation, adaptation and sociological tests, when the individual is ready we allow social interaction without supervision. That man was a friend of one of our patients. He brought the patient out and they brought drugs back in with them. Unfortunately, the friend overdosed.'

I could tell by the worried look on my mother's face that she wasn't going to let me stay here. 'Right, is there someone that I can speak to? Rachael is only fifteen and I'm not happy with this at all.'

'Ma, I'm not staying here. No way,' I interrupted, seeing my chance to escape.

The receptionist looked concerned. 'Of course. Come this way with me, please.' 'Rachael, just wait here for a minute, ok?' my mother pleaded.

I gave them a dirty look and they walked away. The scorching sun was splitting through the tropical palm-trees, but I couldn't get the image of the body-bag out of my head. They can do what they want, there's no way in a million years I'm staying here. I can't believe they're even thinking about it after that happening. I was lost in thought.

'Hey, little woman,' I heard someone say beside me, as a tall man approached me. 'What you doing here? Are you coming to stay with us?' I could recognise the Jamaican accent a mile away.

'Emm, no,' I answered. 'My mother wants me to stay, but I don't want to.'

'Tell me about it. It's not all that bad, you know. I'm Lenny,' he said coolly, offering his hand for me to shake.

'Nice to meet you. I'm Rachael.' Lenny had a kind face with big sad eyes, but I liked him straight away.

'Did you get a chance to look around? It's amazing, you know.'
'No, I just got here.'
'Come on with me and I'll introduce you to my wife.'
'Your wife is here as well?' I was amazed.
'Yeah, we both came from Kingston, but I'm here a bit longer than my wife. You'll have to go easy on her; she's still having a hard time coming off the crack.'

I followed Lenny through the villa, apprehensive about going any further. We passed Mediterranean-looking huts with straw roof-tops. 'This is where we live,' Lenny explained. 'You can either have your own hut or one of the apartments over there.'

I tagged along after Lenny, jumping over a set of concrete lily-pads set into the grass.

'That's where we have therapy,' he said pointing to an outdoor conservatory, 'And here's where we hang out the most.' The swimming pool. I was impressed. 'All together, there's forty acres of land. You can go horse-riding if you want, or play bowling. The alleys are over there.'

I could hear music in the distance. It got louder as we walked towards what appeared to be a restaurant, also outdoor, on stilts. The patients were gathered around the one table as if they were having a meeting. No doubt they're talking about the man who had just died, I thought. They all seemed very serious. Except one woman who was singing along to the reggae music.

'*La musica*, Rose, *por favor*,' one of the others shouted. Rose ignored them, singing louder this time, doing twirls, with a smile on her face.

'That's my wife,' Lenny said, as he turned down the volume of the music. 'Everyone, this is Rachael.' The group glanced at me, nodded and got back to their meeting.

'What have we got here? A white Rastafarian!' Rose said, as she took me by the arm. 'Look at the Robert Marley tattoo on her arm. You're in the right place, girl.' And I was, I thought to myself, looking at the swimming pool and the swaying palm trees. This would be more like a holiday than a detox.

At dinner time my mother and Laurence had found me in the restaurant. 'Well, you seem to be settling in well,' Laurence said with a smile. Laurence was always cracking jokes about my addiction. I think he found it easier to deal with me in this way.

'Listen, Rachael, you only have to stay here for three weeks. Myself and Laurence are going back to Ireland, but we'll come back and collect you then,' my mother assured me. Out of sight, out of mind again. Why didn't my mother just talk to me about my drug problem, instead of bringing me to the other side of the earth, I wondered. But I already knew the answer to that. The usual story, except that now I was in a lot more trouble. I needed her now more than ever.

Leaving me in Cuba only fuelled my sense of abandonment and anger. When I go home, I'm gonna go fuckin' mad. I'll get her back for this, I pledged to myself. I'll definitely get her back. Then I began to panic. 'No, you can't leave me here on my own!' They both looked away and I could feel the tears well up in my eyes. 'I fuckin' hate you,' I shouted, as I stormed away from the restaurant.

I wandered aimlessly around the villa, contemplating making some sort of a getaway, when my thoughts were interrupted by a stream of Spanish. '*Buenos dias, Racquelita. Me llamo Gregorio.* You can call me Greg. *Andamos a la casa.* We go to the house, ok?' Smiling, Greg dragged my suitcases into one of the huts. 'Living room, bathroom, bedroom, ok?' He gave me a smile and left me alone. I opened the wardrobe and climbed inside. I hunched myself up into the foetal position and cried my heart out.

———

The time came for my mother and Laurence to go home. I hadn't spoken to them since we arrived in El Quinque. I hoped that my ma would see sense and change her mind. But she didn't. I was being left in this strange treatment centre with people from Latin America and I couldn't understand a word they were saying. Everyone was much older than me, except for Mauricio and Alejandro, both fifteen years old like me and from Colombia. Alejandro had been a crack user and he could speak a little bit of English. He loved telling me stories of his escapades with the

Colombian Mafia. I put his delusions down to his crack withdrawals.

Mauricio looked like a model and we were attracted to one another straight away. We couldn't communicate, but our attraction didn't need words. It was physical. He was beautifully tanned with a toned body and a boyish, chiselled face. Before long we were sleeping together. Connected by our own pain and troubles, we would lie under the night sky, staring at the stars, wishing we were anywhere but in El Quinque.

Three weeks passed quickly, but there was no sign or word from my mother. She wouldn't accept my phone calls and I was becoming more and more fearful that I would be stuck in Cuba forever. El Quinque was more like a holiday camp than a treatment centre. With very little supervision or guidance from the staff, there were drug-filled parties and orgies every night, which frightened the life out of me. I got the impression that El Quinque was more concerned with the money they were receiving than with the welfare of their patients.

Going to therapy and mixing with the other patients seemed pointless to me. Unlike them, I wasn't an addict: they were a lot worse on the drugs than I ever could be. I didn't need to be in a treatment centre receiving therapy like them. They were all crazy anyway. So I spent most of my time isolated in my room, listening to rave music and fantasising about drugs. The highlight of my day was medication time, when I was pumped up with all sorts of medication while the other patients went to therapy. I was hurting badly and I needed some comfort, so I turned my room into a replica of Ballymun by painting the flats on to my walls, along with paintings of needles and junkies' faces. I tried to soothe my hurt by living in my head and plotting revenge against my mother. But no amount of plotting or eating or having sex with Mauricio could ease my pain. It seemed that the only person I could really talk to was Lenny. He had become my friend and I would talk to him about my family and my life back in Ireland—

I could confide my pain and rage to Lenny and I knew that he understood. But I still felt lonelier than ever. Five months had passed in El Quinque and no-one from Ireland had made any contact, let alone come back to get me. I began to slip into a state of depression.

———

Then one day I heard a familiar voice outside my apartment. '*Racquel, Racquel.*' I couldn't believe it. It was my uncle Laurence. I jumped up off my bed and raced out to give him a big hug. I forgot about everything that had happened in the last five months. Laurence hadn't broken his promise to me, I thought. He had come back to get me.

I was later to learn that the reason I'd been left so long in this place was that Mick's friend 'Donal' had run off with the money and my fees at El Quinque had not been paid. Laurence had to break me out of the place and make a run for it, back to Havana and home, putting his own life at risk for me, terrified that we would get caught. I didn't care about any of this. I was just relieved that I was getting out of this hole and going home.

———

And of course, the 'holiday' in Cuba had been a complete waste of time. My family had got rid of the problem for a few months, but as soon as I saw the flats in Ballymun, my cravings for heroin kicked in. It was as if the previous five months had never happened.

I was surprised to see my old buddies Katie, Emer and Mary, waiting outside my grandmother's house to welcome me back. 'Ah, thank God you're alright,' they all said, their arms wrapped around me in a huge hug, crying their eyes out. 'Just don't start hanging around with all them in Poppintree again. They were the ones who got you into this trouble,' Emer said.

'I won't, I promise,' I agreed, so pleased to see them. 'Is there anyone around with a bit of hash?' I asked them.

'Ah, Rachael, don't start already,' said Katie.

'No, I'm ok, I swear. I'm just stressed out after all that flying. Honestly, I'm grand.'

'Ok…' Katie looked at me suspiciously. 'You'll get some in Sillogue. Knock around to us when you get it.'

I was so excited to be home that I couldn't breathe. 'Ma,' I shouted to my grandmother, 'I'm back.'

I was expecting her to welcome me back with open arms, but instead she came out of the kitchen with a panicked look on her face. Barely pausing to greet me, she followed, 'You needn't unpack your stuff—you're not staying here. You're going to stay in your mother's.'

'Jesus, thanks very much. It's lovely to see you too.'

'You've got to go now. She's waiting for you,' my nanny insisted, looking flustered.

I couldn't believe this. After five months of refusing to talk to me, to even acknowledge my existence, my mother was expecting me to sit down and have a nice chat. 'Is she?' I shouted. 'Yeah, well, I've been waiting for her for five months, so she can wait. I'm going around to Katie's.'

'Don't be long. Herself and Mick are staying in the Westbury and they're waiting for you to meet them for dinner. If you're not back in fifteen minutes, I'll be around to get ye.' Mick liked to stay at the Westbury when he was doing business in Dublin: himself and my mother liked to eat well, dress well and look the part. I was dreading seeing my ma. Now I definitely needed something to calm my nerves. The thought of confronting my ma without something in my system seemed unbearable. I couldn't score gear though. I'd have to wait. Hash wouldn't really hit the spot, but it would have to do for now.

———

My mother and Mick were sitting in the lounge of the hotel waiting for me to arrive. They looked like something from a glossy magazine, she with her thick blonde shiny hair, a simple LBD, a dab of make-up with a touch of scarlet red lipstick. Mick looked equally slick in his immaculate black suit.

'Ah, would you look, the eagle has finally landed,' he said as I approached their table. 'Where's your new boyfriend, Mauricio? I sent him over a ticket so that he could come back with you and stay in Ballymun Hotel,' Mick found himself hilarious. While he would row in when needed and help me out, he often cracked jokes like these at my expense.

I wished I hadn't smoked that joint. I was even more anxious and fidgety and I didn't know how to respond to Mick. 'I heard that he only has one leg, has he?' Mick continued to wind me up.

'No, it's not funny,' I said, as if I were three years old.

'Ah, come on now. Are you not talking to us? I'll tell you what, I'll bring you into town tomorrow and buy you new clothes. That might cheer you up.'

My mother didn't say a word during this exchange and I had no idea of how to talk to her about Cuba. I couldn't ask her why she had dumped me there for five months without a word and why she had refused any contact with me while I was there. So instead I said nothing and went along as if nothing had happened.

At this time, my mother and Mick moved into a new house on the south side of the city. Philip had started in a new school in the area and everyone agreed that it would be in my best interests to go and live with them, away from temptation in Ballymun and my cronies in Poppintree. Mick decided that my rehabilitation was to be a personal project. He took me under his wing. Anywhere he went, I had to go, so that he could keep an eye on me. He got me a job as a waitress in a pub across the road from their house and things seemed to be going well, but having candle-lit dinners and playing happy families with my mother, who seemed like a complete stranger, irritated me. It was as though we were living in the twilight zone, brushing everything under the carpet and pretending things were great, when everything just seemed so fake. I couldn't take it much longer and the first opportunity that I got to run back to Ballymun, I took. I couldn't get heroin out of my head.

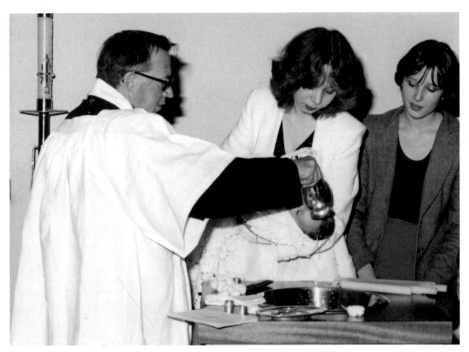

1979. This is my christening photo, the one that my mother, Lynda, tore up. My father should be standing beside my auntie Jacqueline (*right*)—but my mother didn't want me to know who he was.

1986. This is me on my communion day, young, bright and with everything to live for. Little did I know what lay ahead.

1986. With my grandmother Theresa and my brother, Philip. Philip was only a few months old, and I was still trying to get used to the idea of having a brother.

1986. (*Left to right*) My uncle Laurence, my grandfather John and my other uncle Jonathan, taken at my auntie Marion's wedding.

1987. Me and my teddy. When I look at this picture, I wonder how on earth did I go from being so sweet and innocent—to a full-blown heroin addict.

1987. With my brother, Philip. I just loved it when he came to visit. We would spend most of our time playing together.

My brother, Philip, and I again, spending time in my grandparents' garden. I missed him when I was on drugs. But now that I am drug-free we are the best of friends.

1989. This is me studying and being a model student. My homework always came first, before anything else.

1989. My grandparents John and Theresa Keogh. My grandfather taught me about life's difficulties. My grandmother taught me how to love and get through them.

1990. (*Left to right*) My auntie Marion, my mother, Lynda, and my other auntie Jacqueline. This picture was taken during better times, before they knew the extent of my addiction. But even through the tough times they always remained close.

1999. This picture shows how close my grandmother Theresa and I were. It was taken at my auntie Jacqueline's wedding. But my grandmother had to send me home early that night because I was so sick and stoned. My make-up and clothes hid the truth of my addiction.

2000. Here I'm with my auntie Marion and her adopted son, Naladun. The picture was taken just after I had split up with Derek, and it was my first real rock bottom. I was very sick, and I'm convinced now that, if I had not gone to Italy at that stage, I would have died.

2005. A picture that makes me sad. I had just left the Rutland Centre, broken up with Derek—and relapsed. This was when I began to self harm.

2005. In the place that brought me to my knees with drugs: Ballymun.

2005. In Ballymun again—probably getting ready to go shoplifting. Without the clothes and make-up, I looked like death warmed up.

2005. The Ballymun blocks were a comfort to me. Deep down, I thought I didn't deserve any better than the life I was living.

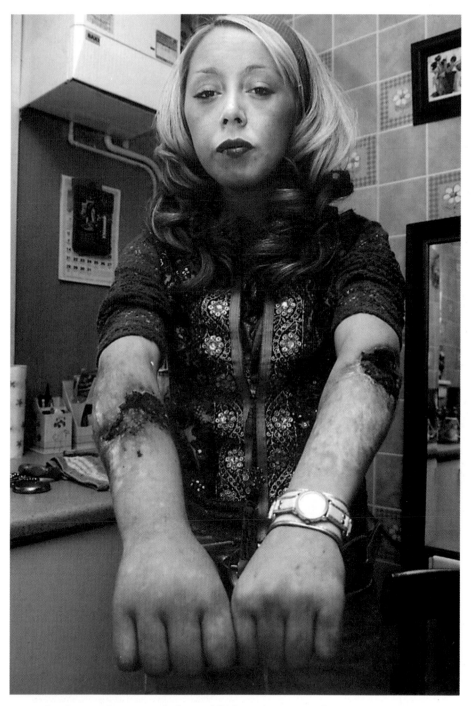

2006. Here I am at the very end of my addiction. I knew in my heart that I couldn't live for much longer.

2006. I had just been released from prison on the recommendation of Dr Brian Sweeney. The media were my life-line, although how I coped with the pressure I will never know.

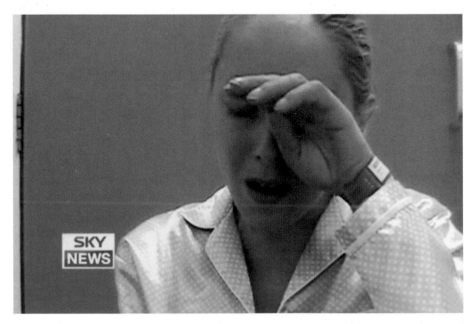

SKY NEWS

2006. At the Mater Hospital, waiting to go into treatment. I was at my lowest ever point—and quickly losing hope.

2006. (*Left to right*) Myself, my brother, Philip, and my mother, Lynda. I was on the road to recovery and waiting to go into treatment. And, I was beginning to build bridges with my family.

2006. Alison O'Reilly, the Sky News reporter (*left*), and myself. Alison believed in me when I couldn't believe in myself.

2007. Here I am, drug-free and heavily pregnant, giving a talk in a school.

My beautiful son, Senán. He was worth it all.

2008. My two great loves: Patrick, and our wonderful son, Senán.

Chapter 7 ∾

| THE DEVIL'S PLAYGROUND

By now Ballymun was infested with drugs. Everyone who had got into the rave scene was now taking heroin. The old-time junkies had been replaced by younger junkies who were taking ownership of the shopping centre and almost every block in Ballymun, claiming their patch of land and openly selling drugs as though they had a licence to do so.

My attraction to drugs was at its peak. I relished doing something that I wasn't supposed to be doing, sticking my two fingers up at my family and the rest of the world and saying, 'Fuck you all, I'll show you and then you'll be sorry.' My appetite for drugs was insatiable—Es, hash, whatever I could get my hands on, and I was no longer getting a buzz out of smoking heroin. Most of my friends were injecting at this stage. They were spending less money than I was and getting more of a stone, so in my twisted logic I thought I might as well join them. I was doing heroin anyway, so I may as well be injecting, I thought.

It was one of my friends who gave me my first 'turn-on'. He took a shine to me and without fail he would give me a whistle any time he passed my house. His eyes would be pinned to the back of his head and I knew that he was injecting heroin. I called him The News of The World, because he knew everyone's business. He was one of these people who never knew when to say goodbye and even when he was miles down the road he would still be shouting at me trying to tell me something.

He brought me to one of his friends' flats to give me a turn-on. I knew that I was playing with fire, but that made me want to do it even more. He put the works into my arm and I felt nothing but a harsh sting. I had crossed the line. I had done the very thing that I thought I would never do. Now there was no going back.

———

As my addiction grew, my grandmother's house became like Fort Knox. If there was something of value that wasn't nailed to the floor, or locked in a room, I would rob it. If it *was* nailed to the floor or locked in a room, I would still find a way to rob it. On occasion I would borrow ladders from the neighbours and climb in through my grandmother's window, taking anything that I could sell for twenty pounds or more. I knew that what I was doing was wrong, but I couldn't let myself think about the consequences of my actions. The drugs came first and I couldn't allow anything to get in my way.

My family was baffled—I might have had my problems, but how on earth could I steal from my grandmother? 'Throw her fucking out,' Laurence would tell my grandmother. 'She's a conniving little bitch and she's just going to keep fleecing us.' Of all my family, my addiction had the strongest effect on Laurence. I had always been close to him and he found it hard to see me like this. He felt responsible in some way for my behaviour and it really began to take its toll on him because he was seeing the worst of it. But I had my grandmother wrapped around my little finger. Even though she knew I was stealing from her, she couldn't bring herself to throw me out, or to disown me. And I knew that if I could get around her, then I would get away with it.

Everyone in the area knew what I was up to. Some of them would even buy my grandmother's jewellery or clothes that she had just bought, even though they knew they were hers. I would tell them that they were shop-lifted, but my grandmother would find out who I sold her stuff to and she would have to buy everything back. Then I would rob and sell them again. By this stage, though, robbing from her wasn't enough. I had to resort to shop-lifting. I couldn't believe how easy it was. Once I didn't appear to be on drugs and I avoided the security cameras, I would usually get away with it. The hard part was selling the stuff around Ballymun without getting caught by the gardaí.

The little garda shop didn't know what hit it. With the nightly drug-induced parties, and drugs being sold on every street corner, they were on high alert. Everywhere I went, I seemed to bump into Garda PJ Walsh and Garda Emily Tormey. They were both working around the clock. They were on a mission: trying to do every drug-addict for something or another, in competition to see who got the most brownie points and convictions. 'There ye are again, Rachael. What's in the bag?' they would say, grinning, as they approached me. I would be kicking myself for getting caught. Over a short period of time, I had used up all my warnings and referrals to the JLO (Juvenile Liaison Officer), so that the gardaí had no choice but to push for a conviction. I was fifteen years old and I was going to Mountjoy Women's Prison.

————

I had no idea what to expect. I had heard some horror stories about the men's Mountjoy and I prayed that the women's prison wouldn't be as bad. Not that the fear of going there had been any deterrent to me stealing and shop-lifting—I couldn't see any further than the turn-on and the blissful feeling of warmth and safety which would follow, the sense that nothing mattered except that moment. What I was more afraid of now was the withdrawals which I would experience while I was in prison, the 'sickness' which addicts like me were in mortal fear of and would do anything to avoid.

I was brought to the prison in what was called the 'dog-box', a two-man metal cage inside a lorry, and I was thankful that I was on my own. After my personal details were given and registered, I was vigorously strip-searched and showered in the reception area and was given my Mountjoy bumper pack, which consisted of a toothbrush, toothpaste, a comb, an old duvet cover and sheet, a couple of pairs of granny knickers with flowers on them, a paper nightdress and a cotton rust-coloured tracksuit. With my hair still wet and my sickness beginning to set in, I was brought into the main section of the prison.

Before me stretched a long, institution-green corridor. It had cells on each side of it, with a barred-off area at the top for the officers, the chief and the governor to work from. I could see two lengthy landings up above and I thought that I would get sick with the fear that was in my stomach.

It was night-time and all the girls were locked in their cells. 'Sorry, Rachael, but you're out of luck,' the prison officer said. 'The place is chock-a-block and there are no empty cells, so we'll have to stick you in the recreation room.' She unlocked the hefty metal door and I couldn't believe what I saw: six women lying on the floor of the television room. 'There ye go. Grab yourself a mattress and make yourself at home,' she said, closing the door behind her and leaving me to my own devices.

'How'ya, love. Here, put your mattress over there. What are ye in for?' one of the women drawled.

'Shop-lifting,' I answered, trying my best to sound common and to not show any fear. 'Is this your first time in here?' another one asked, as though she could smell it off me.

'Yeah.'

'What age are ye?'

'Fifteen.'

'Ah, jaysus, she's only a fuckin' baby. Don't worry love, ye'll be alright. Just don't let anyone take the piss oura ye. Have ye a'in with ye?'

I hadn't a clue what she meant. 'Like wha'?'

'Have ye any gear with ye?'

'No,' I replied, wondering how on earth she thought I'd managed to smuggle gear in with me.

'Yeah, well, if ye get a'in up, just be careful who ye tell. 'Cos it'll be took off ye. Put your name down for the doctor in the morning and he'll give you a sup of phy. (Physeptone was administered to those of us with drug problems, to take the edge off our withdrawals.) Are ye sick now love?' the woman continued, looking at me sympathetically.

'Yeah, a little bit.'

'D'ye want me to massage a bit of Deep Heat into your legs for ye?'

I didn't know what to say. If I said no, she would probably be offended and give me a few digs. If I said yes, she would probably try and feel me up. I decided to go for the few digs. 'Ah, no, it's grand. I'm not that sick anyway.'

'Here, put a bit on us, will ye,' said another woman, pulling up her nightdress to reveal purple, bloated legs.

'Would ye believe she's a great-grandmother. Aren't ye, Kathleen? Practically lives in this place, don't ye, love?' Deep Heat said. 'Ye wouldn't think it, sure ye wouldn't?' Kathleen looked like she was heavily sedated and as though she was a great-grandmother ten times over. 'And that's Maduppa over there in the corner,' Deep Heat continued. 'Here Maduppa, make us a pair of brogues there, will ye, love?' Maduppa appeared to be African. She sat quietly on her own, making shoes out of strips of leather.

There was a girl in the cell whom I recognised from Ballymun. She also seemed heavily sedated. She mentioned a couple of girls from Ballymun whom I knew well and who were also in Mountjoy. 'The two of them are in here, up on the top landing. Ye'll see them in the morning.'

Ah, thank God, I thought. They'll make sure nothing happens to me. That night I fell asleep desperately trying to distract myself from the sound of two of the girls having sex with each other. I was lying right next to them, cringing in my own skin. I just prayed that they wouldn't come near me.

———

'Breakfast time,' I heard someone shout the next morning. I had got through my first night in Mountjoy still intact. I walked out onto the corridor and joined the queue for breakfast. I had never in my life seen so many women in one place, all of them in their pyjamas and slippers, walking around as though they owned the place. Then I noticed one of the girls I knew. She was standing at the top of the queue. I was just about to call her, when some girl marched over and viciously flung a pot of boiling hot water over her. She screamed, but no sound came out. Within seconds the screws were over, dragging both of the girls out of my sight, urging us to get our breakfast and to get back to our cells.

Within days I had moved up to the same landing as my friends from Ballymun. Because I was one of her own, my friend, who sold gear on the outside, made sure that I wasn't left to go through any sickness. I was given fifty mls of Physeptone daily and I quickly settled into life in prison. The majority of women were drug users and got their drugs in through visitors, or sewn into the hem of their clothes. They would anxiously wait in the yard, biting their nails, praying that their visitors wouldn't let them down with the 'dropsy' as it was called. It was as clear as daylight when someone had got drugs in: she would suddenly get an urge to 'clean her cell', then she would disappear for about an hour and come back out to the yard, full of beans, with her eyes pinned to the back of her head.

Life in Mountjoy was a real eye-opener. Most of the lifers, or women who were doing long sentences, had the top landing to themselves, making their cells like little bedsits and getting more privileges than the other women. The second landing was for women in custody, who were usually in on drug-related charges. This landing was more chaotic, with women ripping each other off and having fights daily, each woman trying to make a name for herself and become the top dog. The bottom landing was for women who suffered with their mental health and who were kept on twenty-four hour watch. It was a jungle and even the officers sometimes seemed as intimidating as the inmates.

Prisoners were bursting out of the seams in Mountjoy. Even the library had been made into a sleeping area. Those of us who could were advised by the prison officers to put in an affidavit for temporary release. I had been in Mountjoy for a couple of weeks when I was called to see the Governor, Mr Lonergan. 'You are being granted temporary release, Ms Keogh, on condition that you sign on daily in your local garda station,' he informed me, before continuing: 'Do you realise that you stick out like a sore thumb in here? Most of the women in this prison have been coming in and out all their lives. You're only fifteen and you still have a chance to get yourself off the drugs. I hope I never see you in here again,' he said.

I ran up to my cell, packed my stuff and raced out of Mountjoy, promising myself that I would never touch another drug for as long as I lived.

Chapter 8 ∾

| DESPERATE MEASURES

B
y now I knew in my heart that I was a drug addict, but I
was still convinced that I had the power to control it. I'll
never let that happen again, I thought. I was just careless,
that's all. If I only have a smoke of heroin on the weekends, I'll be
ok. But I couldn't get the taste of heroin out of my mouth or my
mind. From the moment I opened my eyes every morning, the
thought was there, along with an overriding drive within me to
destroy everything in my path. There was a burning anger inside
of me that only heroin could ease.

Within days I was back to my old tricks, hanging around with
Joanne and my friends in Poppintree, avoiding the gardaí like the
plague and stealing anything that we could get our hands on. The
last place that I wanted to go back to was Mountjoy and I knew
that if I shop-lifted again I would get caught. Also, I was being
watched like a hawk in my grandmother's house, but I needed to
find a way to make money. So when an older man, a drug dealer,
asked me to have sex with him in exchange for drugs, I reluctantly
agreed.

As I made my way over to the man's flat, I glanced up at
Joanne's window to make sure she couldn't see where I was going.
Once again I was out of my own body, watching my feet carry me
towards the door, disconnected from the fact that this was me. He
was happy to see me and wasted no time taking me into his
bedroom. He handed me a lump of heroin in a bag, then asked me

to undress. 'It's alright, chicken, relax. C'mon over and lie down beside me,' he urged.

I wanted to vomit, but I did as he said. With a look of hunger in his eyes he began to touch me in places that made my skin crawl. Then, like a dog, he climbed up on top of me and had sex with me. I lay there with my eyes closed, holding the heroin tightly in my hand and trying to focus on anything but the reality of what was happening. Within minutes it was over and I left his flat, feeling disgusted with myself.

———

My addiction was taking its toll on my family, particularly on my grandparents and on my uncle Laurence. I was robbing them blind, sneaking other drug addicts into my house and using drugs in my bedroom. My grandfather and Laurence began to drink more because of the stress and my grandmother was beginning to look ill. I was angry with Laurence for leaving me in Cuba and he was angry at me for going back on drugs. We would pass each other on the street without any acknowledgment. I was no longer afraid of my grandfather. I would hear him coming in from the pub, hoping he would start a fight so that I could vent all my pent-up anger on him. My aunts had moved out of home and they now began to avoid coming to visit. They knew they would only hear bad news and see my grandmother upset. I was blind to the damage I was doing and I couldn't think of anything but my next fix. My grandmother got tired of my apologies and my promises to get clean. She had no choice but to throw me out of the house.

I was seventeen, and four years had passed since I first started to use heroin. I now lived on the streets with the other junkies, squatting in flats in Ballymun. My life was rapidly falling down around me. Even though I knew I had a problem, I still thought that I could stop whenever I wanted to. I just didn't want to, that was all. I was comfortable with the other junkies. They didn't pester me with encouragements to do better with my life. Most of the time they didn't even want to talk with me. We were all there for the same reason and that was to use drugs.

Around this time, Ballymun got the nickname 'The Devil's Playground'. A society unto itself, hemmed in by seven towers, magnetic to junkies. But there was talk on the streets of a drought, a massive cut-back of drugs that would make it nearly impossible to score heroin. Some dealers were sitting on their heroin, in case they needed it themselves. Others were selling bags for double the usual price, forty pounds, and making a fortune for themselves. Junkies from all over Ireland were making their way to Ballymun in the hope of buying drugs, congregating in the blocks, hunched over and huddled together in the cold, with their hoods pulled up and a manic look in their eyes. Cursing the dealers for leaving them waiting so long, dying sick. As soon as the dealer came he would suddenly become everyone's best friend. Most times the dealers wouldn't have enough heroin for everyone. It was first come first served and usually fights would break out among the junkies.

The residents of the blocks wouldn't let their kids out to play for fear that they would stumble upon someone with a needle in their arm, or even overdosed. They decided to start up an anti-drugs campaign, which was run by no-nonsense vigilantes. They decided to take the law into their own hands and were willing to go to great lengths to clean up Ballymun. It had very little effect. Even when the vigilantes marched on drug dealers' houses, the dealer would just move up the road and sell from there. By now, the drought had got so bad that drug addicts were handing themselves into prison, where they would be guaranteed Physeptone.

At this time, I was in a relationship with a young man named Peter. He had saved me one day from being ripped off, and at such a dangerous time, when I was living on the streets, he was just what I needed, someone to protect me and possibly to keep my habit going. Peter was around six foot tall, well built, with a scar going right down his face. People were afraid of him. Even dealers would run when they saw him coming. They knew he would take all their drugs off them, leaving them with a bag or two if he liked them. Peter and I became like hobos, laying our heads wherever we could and sometimes resorting to sleeping under the stairs in the tower blocks, wrapping ourselves in cardboard boxes and nestling into each other for body heat and to block out the over-powering smell of urine. I was oblivious to everything, injecting all sorts of drugs into my body, from heroin to cocaine, duck-egg tablets, to Benzodiazepine and Napps, anything to take away the pain of how petty my life had become.

Sometimes I would spend the day on my own, endlessly walking the streets in the rain, feeling so sorry for myself and wondering how I had got myself into this mess. My grandparents were adamant about showing me some tough love, closing the door on my face, looking torn apart as I cried on the door-step, begging them to let me back in and give me one more chance. Then one bitterly cold night I had nowhere to go. My only option was to break into my grandparents' shed and sleep in the dog kennel with the dog. My grandfather found me the next morning and gave in to me, picking me up and carrying me back into their house.

It was around this time that I began to get heavily into taking tablets. Especially Dalmane, because I could easily inject it and mix it up with heroin. Dalmane strongly enhanced the buzz of heroin and made me feel like I was invisible and wrapped up in cotton wool. The downside was that I was a recipe for disaster, getting myself into all sorts of trouble because I was so out of it. My grandmother was a nervous wreck. She never knew whether I would burn us all alive while I goofed off during the night smoking cigarettes in bed. Other times I would goof off right in front of her, defying gravity with my head inches away from the floor or my dinner. I would swear that I hadn't taken anything. 'I'm not on drugs. I'm just thinking of something,' I would tell her.

My nanny's patience and her health were running thin. She was sick of sticking up for me, only for me to let her down over and over again. She was tired of all my tricks, my bullying her for money, emotionally blackmailing her into believing that I could die from withdrawals if I didn't use heroin, trying to convince her that I owed money to people and that they would do terrible things to me if I didn't get them their money, making her feel as guilty as possible by telling her that if I got locked up it would be her fault. She was the one person who loved me and believed in me the most, but she was beginning to see very clearly the person that I had become. I was the complete opposite to what she had always hoped for. I was a junkie, just like my father, and when I looked into her eyes I knew that I was finished.

————

So, when my mother's boyfriend, Mick, asked me if I would go into treatment, I readily agreed. I wasn't ready to give up drugs, but I wanted to make amends to my family and to make some kind of effort to get clean. Mick had made it his mission in life to help me get clean and make a good life for myself. Admittedly, he sometimes did it in unorthodox ways. Firstly he tried to side with me by buying me drugs—preferring to ensure that I was safe taking them than in some dingy shooting den. He would ring me in my grandmother's house and ask me if I was sick. I always said yes, even if I wasn't. Then he would meet me at the shops and give me money to go and score. We would drive to the nearest beach and he would watch me while I had a smoke or a turn-on, asking me what the big deal was about heroin and why I couldn't just have a drink. Then he would try to level with me, asking me why I was doing this to myself. I couldn't answer because I didn't know the answer myself.

Sometimes Mick would bring me up to Benburb Street and show me where the prostitutes worked. 'That's what you'll end up like, if you keep doin' gear,' he would say.

'Yeah right, that's one thing I'll never do,' I insisted, comparing myself to some of the girls and thinking that I was above all that.

'Ah, yeah, I'm sure that's what they all said.'

'Well it won't be me,' I assured him, convinced of what I was saying, selectively forgetting about the fact that I had already sold my body for drugs.

The day came for my assessment and I was accompanied to the Rutland Centre by my mother and Mick. Mick introduced me to one of his friends, Big Mick, who was a recovering addict and had been through the Ruts himself. He met us at the gates of the treatment centre and guided us up the lengthy driveway and towards a Georgian house. He could have passed for a copper, standing at about six foot two with a beefy build. His hair was fair and fell around his face like a pair of curtains. He had his dog, Roxy, with him and I couldn't believe my eyes when he lay on the pebbled ground and began to roll around and howl along with Roxy. His playfulness immediately broke the ice and made me feel comfortable.

After convincing the Rutland that I was ready for treatment, they agreed to take me in the day after my seventeenth birthday, but only if I could find a way to get clean first. The two Micks decided to bring me to Co. Mayo to go through my detox. I bought some methadone, which would help me to come off the heroin without too much withdrawal. The three of us stayed in a B&B while I weaned myself off the heroin and eventually off the methadone. Big Mick kept me distracted from my craving for drugs by acting silly and slagging everyone off in Mayo. He was a big child in a man's body and I was so glad of his company. I didn't realise then that Mick would come to play a huge part in my life and that I would come to owe him so much.

I had just turned seventeen and I was completely drug-free and ready to go into treatment. What I wasn't ready for was to do it for myself. I was entering treatment to keep my family happy; to do what they so desperately wanted for me, but not to give up drugs for my own life or sanity.

My six weeks in treatment flew past in a haze of twice-daily group therapy, where counsellors, nurses and clients alike spoke in a language that was alien to me, a language in which they openly talked about their feelings and how different things affected them. As far as I was concerned, they were all a pack of weirdos. I was told I had the disease of addiction, whatever the hell that was, which meant that I could never, ever again take drugs or any other mood-altering substance without it having serious consequences. I had an addictive personality; I was the kind of person who would get addicted to anything if it helped me to escape from myself and from reality. The drugs weren't the real problem, they told me, *I* was.

I wasn't one bit happy to hear this. The fuckin' cheek of them, I thought. Seventeen years of age and they're telling me that I can't even drink. I don't think so. But I played along, for my family's sake, telling them what I thought they wanted to hear.

However, I didn't get away with it. My two group counsellors, Jimmy and Marie, could see right through my façade and they had no qualms about exposing me in front of the clients in my group. 'Take off the mask, Rachael, and get real,' Marie would say. Then I would start crying.

'Are you upset now because you've been exposed?' she would prompt me.

'No, I'm upset because I can't take this any more,' I would protest.

'So you're feeling sorry for yourself, are you?' Marie had hit the nail on the head, but I wasn't about to admit it.

'No, I just feel terrible over everything that I've done,' I lied, when really I wanted to tell her to fuck off and to stop picking on me. Jimmy and Marie continued to chip away at my so-called denial and I just went along with everything they said.

Narcotics Anonymous meetings were held twice weekly and it was compulsory for me to go. The NA crowd were another group I couldn't get my head around, recovering addicts who claimed to have a life beyond their wildest dreams. And apparently they achieved this by staying abstinent from drugs and working a twelve-step programme. I couldn't fathom for the life of me how sitting around talking about my problems would give me a life beyond my wildest dreams.

'Just for today, you never have to use drugs again,' they would say. So if it's just for today, does that mean that I can use drugs tomorrow? I thought. I found a loop-hole in nearly everything they said. Ninety meetings in ninety days, they suggested. Get a sponsor and use your sponsor. And no matter what happens, DON'T PICK UP DRUGS. Even if your arse falls off you, just don't use. They spoke of NA being a spiritual programme and the importance of having a higher power in their lives. Then at the end of the meeting, we would all stand in a circle, with our arms around one another's shoulders and say the serenity prayer. Then everyone would shout in unison: 'It works if you work it, it won't if you don't, so work it, you're worth it.' I would be dying to laugh and I came to the conclusion that NA was a cult, trying to brainwash me. Sure they probably weren't even drug addicts, I told myself. They were more like sad cases who had nothing better to be doing with themselves than giving me a hard time.

CP day also went right over my head. 'Concerned Persons' day offered friends or relatives the opportunity to come and tell the group how they had been affected by their loved one's or friend's addiction. Laurence came to see me and gave me a right earful in front of the group. He brought everything out in the open: about how I had robbed his clothes and sold them, how I had stolen his girlfriend's gold ring and the arguments that had caused between the two of them; the trip to Cuba and how it left him devastated. I was an ungrateful little bitch, he said, and I was full of shit. He was right. I *was* full of shit, but I wasn't ready to see it.

———

Before I knew it, I had a needle in my arm again. But going to the Rutland had awoken something inside of me, an awareness of myself that had disappeared years earlier. I could no longer use drugs in peace. Maybe the counsellors were right. Maybe *I* was the problem and not the drugs, I wondered. Why did I keep going back to the drugs, then? It must be because there was something wrong with me. Maybe *I'm* the one who's a weirdo, I thought to myself. Oh my God, I'm a weirdo and everybody knows. That's why nobody wants to know me any more. My head would race when I lay in my bed, night after night. And no matter how much drugs I used, I couldn't get away from it.

I needed answers. I had to find out what was wrong with me, so I decided to read every book about addiction that I could get my hands on. I thought that if I could find out what was missing inside of me, I could resolve the problem myself and then maybe I could be like everyone else and have a social drink and a few lines of cocaine. But reading books gave me no answers. It only made me more fearful and analytical and ultimately pushed me further into the drugs.

——

Drug addicts were beginning to drop like flies in Ballymun. The heroin was taking its toll and lots of people were overdosing and dying. I knew that I could be next, but it was a chance I was willing to take. I didn't want to die, but the thought of living without drugs frightened me even more. Sometimes I would see my old friends driving around in their new cars and getting on with their lives. I cursed them and I cursed myself for this affliction. I couldn't bear being in my own skin, so I tried to soothe myself by shop-lifting the best of clothes, jewellery and make-up. If I looked good on the outside, then people wouldn't think I was that bad.

By now I was well known to the gardaí. Every couple of weeks they would raid my grandmother's house for stolen goods or to take me into custody. But then things became so bad that I got arrested for robbing blocks of cheese and rashers from the local shop. It put a real dent in my pride when I stood in front of the judge and the garda insisted on reading out the charge as loudly as possible. I could hear people laughing at the back of the court. I was ashamed and embarrassed.

'Do you have anyone to stand bail for you?' asked my solicitor.

'Yeah, that's my step-da down the back. He'll do it,' I replied. But this time, Mick refused to do anything for me. I was put in custody and sent to Mountjoy.

As soon as I arrived I was told that I had visitors. It was the two Micks. They thought it was all hilarious. 'Blocks of cheese and packets of rashers. Ah, that's the best one yet. What were you trying to do? Feed the whole of Ballymun?' my stepfather said, laughing away to himself.

'What do you want?' I asked, freaked out that they hadn't put up my bail and now they were making a mockery of me.

'Right, this is the deal,' Mick said. 'I'll go bail for you, if you come back to the house to your mother. If you stay clean for a week, I'll bring you over to Texas. But you have to be willing to stay there on your own. And I'll send you money over every month for living expenses.'

'Are you serious?' I said in disbelief. 'Why Texas?'

'Well,' Mick replied, 'you don't seem to be able to get clean over here. I have friends in Texas who are willing to put you up, but they don't know anything about drugs, so you'll have to go through your withdrawals before you go over. Myself and Big Mick will stay with ye for a week, just to make sure you're alright with the whole thing. So what do you think?'

Well, Texas sounded far-fetched to say the least, but then I'd rather go anywhere than Mountjoy, I thought. 'Yeah, I'll do it.'

Going to Texas was different from going to Cuba for me in that I had fully consented to the idea, but only because it was my only option. And Mick seemed to be going to great lengths to ensure my recovery—albeit several thousand miles away.

I stayed with my mother for one week and within those seven days I was over the worst of my withdrawals. Myself and the two Micks flew to Arlington, Texas. I had never thought that I would see myself in Texas. The only ideas I had of Texas came from watching *Dallas* on television. I was excited about meeting some real-life cowboys and starting off afresh, in a place where nobody knew about my past or my addiction. Perhaps this was my chance to leave it all behind me, I reasoned, conveniently forgetting that I had had a number of chances already.

The two Micks had arranged to come with me to Texas and then leave after a couple of days, once I had settled in. When we arrived at the airport, a woman called Susan was waiting for us. She was from Belfast and her father and Mick were old friends. She told me that I would be staying with herself and her other friend Hannah in Fort Worth. Susan was in her late twenties and she had been living in Texas for eight years. She seemed friendly and down-to-earth and she promised me that she would take good care of me, thinking that I was simply coming to Texas for a few months for an extended holiday. She knew nothing of the real reason for my visit. Susan brought me to my new house and introduced me to Hannah, who was older, thirty-nine, and she had been born and raised in Fort Worth. Her big mop of brown hair went right down her back and her face was caked with make-up.

Both Susan and Hannah worked during the day selling property, so most of my time was spent lounging in the garden alone, worshipping the sun and drinking piña coladas. I had no transport so sometimes I would spend hours walking around the neighbourhood, people-watching and wondering if their lives were as perfect as they seemed. The novelty of living in Texas quickly wore off and it wasn't long before the boredom began to sink in. I was getting home-sick and I couldn't help but think that I was missing out on something in Ballymun.

If Mick had hoped that my visit to Texas might make me forget about drugs, it had quite the opposite effect. Sometimes I would hide in my bedroom and I would tightly wrap a tourniquet around my arm, feeling a sense of nostalgia as I watched my veins come to the surface, trying to burst through my skin. Then I would fantasise about my next turn-on. The anticipation of scoring heroin, the stimulation of getting that little bag of brown into my hand and doing what I wasn't supposed to be doing. I would find a place where I wouldn't be disturbed, then I would put on some music like Pink Floyd or David Bowie, just to add to the tragedy of it all. I would mix the heroin with the citric acid, burn underneath the spoon and watch in delight as they blended and bubbled together to form a dark brown liquid. My mouth would water as I thought about getting the vein and seeing the blood enter the barrel. Then I would thrust the heroin into my body, feeling like every part of me was being oiled. I would taste the heroin on the back of my mouth and I would slowly drift away from reality.

I wanted to run out of Hannah's house there and then and score drugs, but I was only tormenting myself. I was in a country where I hadn't seen one drug addict and I had no idea of where to find one. Then I thought of Narcotics Anonymous. I had heard that they had meetings all over the world, especially in America. If I wanted to get drugs, surely I would meet someone there that was still using. Maybe they could tell me where to go. Within days I had found a meeting nearby, but I was disgusted to find that they were all really serious about getting clean and staying clean. I couldn't believe how different the meetings were from the ones in Ireland. At one meeting, a man stood on a podium, talking enthusiastically about his experiences and his strength and hope in recovery. I froze on my chair when I realised that he was randomly pointing people out of the crowd and asking them to share. I contemplated doing a runner for the nearest exit, but I was too afraid to move, so I picked a spot on the floor and I kept my eyes firmly on it. If I didn't see him, hopefully he wouldn't see me. I had a lucky escape and I decided that I would never go near NA again.

I had made some new friends who worked in the petrol station near Hannah's house. Caroline was from the Philippines and Anton was from Mexico. They were both really pleasant and welcoming, making it their business to get to know me. At first I wondered why they were so nice, but then I realised that it was just their way. I wasn't used to people being nice just for the sake of it. Anton was so fond of me that he began to give me free bottles of alcohol, just because I was Irish and therefore I was more than likely an alcoholic, he reasoned. Spending time with them both became the highlight of my day. Every Saturday I would visit Caroline's house. She lived with her mother and her two aunts, who couldn't speak a word of English. Caroline's mother and aunts acted as though I wasn't even there, but sat at the table playing cards and shouting aggressively at one another. Myself and Caroline would have our own little party, drinking bottles of Ritz and attempting to sing karaoke. I would get so drunk that I would pass out and somebody would have to drive me home. It seemed that, for the meantime, alcohol would do as a replacement for the drugs I craved.

Hannah was beginning to get worried. She sat me down one day and asked me what was going on. I told her all about my past and my addiction, how I couldn't stop thinking about drugs and how lonely I was. She cried as she listened to me and from then on she became like my big sister, minding me and bringing me everywhere she went. She even brought me to her workplace at a set of condos. She would sit in her office and I would lie by the pool. Hannah introduced me to a young man called Josh, thinking that he would be good company for me. Josh was a nice, old-fashioned, salt-of-the-earth kind of guy, good looking in a strait-laced and clean-cut type of way. Not someone that I would usually hang-out with, but I liked him. He would take me to the cinema or to one of the giant shopping malls in the area, acting like a gentleman and being on his best behaviour. One day he took me to meet his grandmother. She was a little old lady who was proud of her grandson. We both sat together drinking iced tea as Josh played 'Hey Jude' on the piano. It was so nice that I wanted to puke. I didn't like or trust people who were this happy and it completely turned me off Josh. I spent weeks not answering his phone calls, hoping that he would get the hint and get lost. He eventually did and I kind of felt sorry for him but he just wasn't exciting enough for me.

———

Susan had just broken up with her boyfriend, Will, a soldier in the American army whom Susan liked to call her 'big teddy bear'. But they were no longer on speaking terms and Susan wanted to celebrate her new-found freedom by going out nightclubbing with me. I was delighted to have myself a new drinking buddy and, after getting myself some fake ID, we both went on the rip. We decided to go to a line-dancing club. I was amazed when I saw everyone dressed in their cowboy suits, dancing together in what appeared to be a bull ring. After a few glasses of vodka and coke and a couple of shots of Tequila, I found myself in the middle of it all. Myself and Susan danced for hours, making our way up on to tables and making a holy show of ourselves.

When it was time to go home, I suggested that we take a lift from one of her friends. But Susan was getting more aggressive by the minute and she insisted that she drive home herself. No matter what I said to her, she just wouldn't listen. I couldn't let her go home on her own, so I decided to get in the car with her. Susan seemed to be driving safely and within minutes I fell asleep. I was woken by an ear-splitting screech. All I saw was us heading full force into the back of a pick-up truck. I felt my seat-belt tighten around my torso as we made contact. Then everything went blank. When I woke up I was in the hospital. I had been kept there until I sobered up. I had got away with bruised lungs, but the police were waiting to question me. After being breathalysed I had no choice but to admit that I had been drinking. They gave me a warning and informed me that Susan was being held in custody and she would be charged with drinking and driving.

I felt terrible. Even though Susan had insisted on driving, I had egged her on in her drinking and partying, delighted to have a drinking buddy at last. I couldn't help wondering if I was partly responsible. Was I the kind of person who brought negativity and bad things with her wherever she went, infecting others and making terrible things happen? I tortured myself with the thought.

The next day Susan was brought to court and she was put on two years' probation. I never saw her again.

———

When it was time for me to return to Ireland, as my visa had expired, Hannah brought me to the airport. We had both become really close, especially since Susan moved out. Hannah had been so understanding and supportive to me since I opened up to her and neither of us wanted to say goodbye. But I missed Ireland and I was ready to go home, even though I knew in my heart that I was going to use drugs as soon as I got the chance. But I also knew in my heart that I no longer had control over my drug use. Texas had been a waste of time. I had merely substituted drink for the drugs.

I realised that my using drugs always had consequences but they weren't bad enough to make me want to stop.

Anyway, when my back was against the wall I could always count on my family to send me on a little holiday. In fact, they seemed only too keen to do so, I thought. They were probably delighted to see the back of me for a bit. My new motto had become, 'Go on heroin and see the world'. Who knows, maybe next time they'll send me to Thailand or even better, Afghanistan, I thought.

Chapter 9 ❧

| TRUE FRIENDS?

I was still only seventeen and underneath my sarcasm and jokes about my life I was really hurting and was desperately lonely. I was living with my grandmother again and I missed my mother and my brother Philip. I wanted nothing more than to be part of the family. Philip was ten years of age and I loved when he came to visit my grandparents. Sometimes I would watch him playing around the house and it would hit me that I had only been three years older than him when I'd first started to use heroin. Other times I couldn't stand the idea of being around him, because I felt so ashamed of who I had become. I wished that I could just talk to my mother and tell her how I felt, but my fear of her rejecting me if I did was far too great for me to take the risk. And my fear of her not rejecting me seemed even worse, because then she wouldn't be the problem, *I* would. It was easier for me to talk to my grandmother. I could just be myself with her and I knew that no matter what I did, she wouldn't reject me.

I slowly began to open up to my grandmother about my addiction. I admitted to her that I had a problem with the drugs. I told her that I really wanted to stop, but I didn't know how. She was just as baffled as I was. Sometimes she would cry and express her frustration at not being able to help me. Mostly she would just say, 'Don't worry, you'll be grand.'

I am not sure if she really believed this, but I was far from grand. I was becoming more attracted to drugs and the lifestyle that it brought. From the moment that I opened my eyes in the morning until I closed them that night, I was consumed with thoughts of heroin. I was in the grip of the drug and I was losing the fight to stay sane and healthy.

One of the side-effects of taking heroin is that you make friends with all kinds of people simply because you are both using. But these friendships are often far from healthy, as both of you are coming from a place of desperation, need and deception. Cindy was one of these 'friends' for me. I met her in a friend's flat, which had been turned into a using gallery. Every room would be occupied by junkies, floating around the place like shadows, endlessly searching for beauty in each hit.

Cindy began to show her face every night at two or three in the morning. A strange time to be scoring some heroin, I thought. She wasn't like any junkie I had met before. She was of mixed race, healthy looking and very confident in herself, chatting away to everyone as if she had known them all her life. She had only just moved into Ballymun with her boyfriend and her two young children. She told us that her boyfriend didn't know she was using, so every night when he went to sleep she had to sneak out and go and score.

We got on like a house on fire and it wasn't long before she invited me over to her flat and asked me to babysit. Her flat was spotless and well kept, totally unexpected from someone who was using drugs. There was no sign of her boyfriend. I never asked her where she was going when I babysat, but when she came back she would sit in front of me and count wads of money. Then she would take out eight bags of heroin, each bag with its one score: four for me and four for her.

One night she told me where she was getting the money from. 'I was up in Coronation Street,' she said when she came back to the flat. I looked at her blankly. 'On the egg and mash, you know, on the game.' I had my suspicions anyway, but I pretended to be surprised. Then she told me that she had split up with her boyfriend, because he had found out about her using drugs.

From then on, babysitting for Cindy became a nightly thing. She would go out working at about eleven and she would be home by two or three. It was as though nothing had happened. She looked great, she seemed content, her flat was beautiful, her kids were angels. She wasn't short of money and she always had drugs. It all seemed so easy and I began to get curious.

'You just have to look at it like a job,' Cindy assured me. 'Never allow your emotions to get in the way and never bring your work home with you. If you want, you can come into Baggot Street with me. You don't have to do anything, just see what you think.'

I was more than reluctant. I had promised myself that I would never do anything like this again, especially after the last time. But then I had promised myself lots of things that I could never seem to follow through. I was attracted to what Cindy had—all that money and access to all the drugs she wanted—and I was attracted to what I saw as the danger of it all. I wouldn't do anything, I told myself. I would just go with Cindy and see what it was like.

We got the last bus into town and headed up to Baggot Street. That was where the real money was, with the majority of clients being wealthy businessmen. But it wasn't what I had expected. There were no women strutting their stuff in mini-skirts and whore boots, fighting over who owned what patch. Cindy told me that most of the women had already done their work and had finished up for the night.

We stood together at the banks of the canal and every few minutes a car would crawl towards us. The driver would stare out the window, trying to get a good look at us both. Cindy approached the first car that stopped. I could see her leaning in through the window, negotiating terms. Then she jumped into the car and they drove off. I hid in the shadows praying that nobody would drive past who knew me. Baggot Street was dark and eerie, like a ghost-town, and I shuddered when I remembered stories I had heard of prostitutes getting beaten up by punters.

Cindy was back within forty minutes. 'How much did ye make?' I asked her as soon as she got out of the car.

'Eighty pounds,' she said proudly.

'And what did you do?'

'I done the business with him.'

'No way, and what do you say to the punter? Do you talk to him or anything?'

Just as I said this, a van pulled up beside us. 'C'mon over with me and I'll show you,' she said linking my arm and taking me with her. 'Are ye looking for business?' she asked the driver, who looked like a rabbit caught in the headlights. I was surprised to see that he was very young. Maybe in his late twenties. Not a dirty old man like I'd expected.

'What, with the two of you?' he asked.

'Yeah, there's coffee and cream on the menu tonight if you want it. I'm coffee and she's cream.' I gave Cindy an elbow into the ribs.

'How much are ye looking for?'

'Depends on what you want.'

'Well what's the price list?'

'It's a hundred and sixty for sex, eighty for a blow-job and sixty for a hand-job.'

'I'll give you the one sixty,' he agreed.

'Wait! Hold on for a minute,' I interrupted, pulling Cindy to one side. 'What the fuck are you doing?' I said, exasperated.

'Look, if you're gonna do this,' Cindy responded, 'you may as well do it with me there. You'll feel safer that way. And I'll do most of the work. You just have to go along with me.'

'Ah, I don't know about this, Cindy. It's a bit weird and I'm fuckin' freaked out.'

'We'll make this the last one,' she assured me. 'I have eighty here and we'll get one sixty off him. So we'll have enough to do us for tomorrow as well.'

I quickly weighed up the options in my head. I couldn't think of another way to make money this quick. 'Fuck it, c'mon then,' I reluctantly agreed, letting all my morals go out the window. 'Just this once won't kill me.'

We got into the back of the man's van and brought him somewhere out of sight. 'I have to get the money off you first,' Cindy told him. He did as she said, producing a bundle of notes out of his jeans pocket. Then the punter pulled down his jeans and he began to touch himself as he hungrily watched myself and Cindy undress. Even though I had lots of drugs in my system, every part of me screamed out, telling me not to do this. But I couldn't just walk away now. I had gone too far and, anyway, it would all be over in a few minutes. I couldn't look at either of them. I suddenly burst out laughing, to relieve the tension I felt inside. Then Cindy started to laugh, too.

'What are you laughing at?' the punter said, obviously freaked out.

'Sorry, I'm not laughing at you. It's just that this is my first time doing anything like this.'

Cindy went over to the man and had sex with him. She seemed to magically bring him to orgasm within minutes. La la la la la, this isn't happening, I repeated in my head, not knowing where to look and trying to distract myself from how bizarre it all was. When she finished with him, he decided that he had had enough. I was never so relieved.

———

I have no memory of my second time selling my body for money, or the time after that. I was eighteen years old and living the seedy life of a prostitute. But somehow, I managed to switch myself off every time I went to Baggot Street. I became someone different. Someone who was confident and in control, quickly learning all the tricks of a prostitute: relying on my sexuality to get what I wanted and using my body, my facial expressions and how I spoke as my main source of attraction. It always worked. Within a few weeks I had regular customers. All sorts of men paid me to have sex with them. Young, old, middle-class and upper-class, married men and single men. But all their faces looked the same to me. They were a means to an end that came hand in hand with my addiction. It was as though I were living a double life.

I desperately tried to keep it a secret from my family and the rest of the world. At first I would always make sure that I got back into my grandparents' house before my grandmother finished her nightly shift at Dublin Airport. My skin would be crawling with shame as I snuck in the back door and crept up to my bedroom. I would count my money, making sure that I had at least three hundred pounds. Enough to buy gear to last me for two or three days at a time. I was beginning to realise that the more I sold my body for drugs, the bigger my drug habit became. As it began to get bright outside, I would have a turn-on and fall asleep until the next evening.

But I was starting to get very sloppy and very greedy, wanting to make more money every time I went to Baggot Street and staying out until much later. Sometimes when I got home my grandmother would be standing in the kitchen. She would see the taxi pulling off and she would question where I had been. 'You're on the game, aren't you?' she would bluntly say. But I always denied it, knowing that the thought of it devastated her.

Another 'friend' at this time was Derek, who had just appeared out of nowhere in Cindy's flat. I knew his face to see around Ballymun and I wondered what he was doing there after I heard him saying he was clean. He explained that he was doing his rounds with people, collecting money that he was owed from the time he dealt in drugs. He gave me his number and told me to ring him if I ever needed any help getting clean. I was immediately attracted to what I saw as his strength and self-assurance. Little did I know that meeting Derek would be one of the biggest mistakes of my life. Being a drug addict does not mean that you choose your friends with care: you meet all sorts of people, generally in the same boat as you, and trust doesn't exactly come into it. So, when Derek's unpredictable and moody met my desperate and vulnerable, it was an accident waiting to happen.

A few days after meeting Derek I woke up in the Mater Hospital after overdosing on heroin and tablets. My clothes were wringing wet from sweat. I had been given a heroin antidote, but I was screaming at the doctors to give me something to take away the withdrawals. The doctors refused to give me anything and they discharged me as soon as my grandmother arrived. By the time I got home I had lapsed back into another overdose. I was kept in hospital for a few days and the break from drugs gave me that chance to think clearly for the first time in a long while.

I needed to get clean. And I decided to ring Derek to ask him to help me do a detox. He was only too happy to take me under his wing and within one week I was clean from drugs and in a steady relationship with him. Derek was small but stocky. He had shovels for hands and big, square shoulders. He understood me like nobody else did and he made me feel very safe. But there was something about his piercing blue eyes that made me think twice about him. I saw a craziness in them that didn't match up to the person that he presented himself to be: strong and steady. But I just pretended to myself that my instincts were wrong.

A lot of my friends knew Derek and were shocked to hear that he was my new boyfriend. 'What the fuck are you doing with him?' an old Ballymun friend asked me one day. 'I was locked up with him and I'm telling you now, he's not what he seems to be.'

But I wasn't willing to listen. I was introduced to Derek's family who welcomed me in with open arms and within a little time myself and Derek were shacked up together in his mother's sitting room. It was us against the world, pledging loyalty to each other until the day we died. I had never felt safer or more secure in my life.

But soon, Derek began to show me his more unpredictable side. It seemed that my friends were right.

One night we were lying in bed. I was fast asleep, but woke with a start, to find Derek standing over me, staring at me. His eyes glittered.

'What are you looking at me for?' I said, startled.

He shook his head. 'Oh, I'm sorry, I didn't mean it. I was having a bad dream.'

I looked at him doubtfully. 'You weren't even asleep.' I pretended that I needed to go to the toilet. Looking at my face in the bathroom mirror, the first thing I thought of was heroin. I had been clean since I had moved in with Derek, so it would be impossible to use drugs with him around. When I came back downstairs Derek was fast asleep. Now was my opportunity to go and score.

I snuck out of Derek's house and knocked in to Cindy. But she wasn't in and I assumed that she was in Baggot Street. I decided to follow her in, knowing that I would have to do some work myself and be back before Derek woke up.

It was a busy night and I wasn't waiting long for my first client to come. I had never seen this punter before, but he insisted that he was a regular visitor to Baggot Street. He looked like a Goth, with wavy shoulder-length hair, pale skin and lots of eye-liner. After he agreed to pay me for sex, I brought him to my usual hide-out by the docks of the canal. I was just about to unbutton his jeans when he pushed my hand away. 'I have a special request for you,' he said in a posh Dublin accent.

Ah, here we go, another freak, I should have known, I thought to myself, becoming afraid. I watched his hands like a hawk and cursed myself for not having a weapon with me. Then he reached under the seat of his car and pulled out a pair of leather trousers and a pair of women's high-heeled boots. 'I don't want to have sex with you if that's ok. I would much prefer it if you put these boots on and just stood on me,' he said.

'Emm, are you serious?' I replied, incredulous.

'Yeah, that's what I like.'

'Ok, but you'll have to pay me more,' I told him, knowing that he was just as afraid of me as I was of him. He agreed and handed me one hundred pounds. Then he put his leathers on over his jeans.

'You'll have to tell me what to do,' I said, squashing my feet into the stiletto boots. 'As hard as you can, press your feet into my crotch area,' he instructed.

I reluctantly obliged.

'Do it harder,' he demanded and as I obliged, he began to make little purring noises. 'Meeow, meeow,' just like a kitten. I thought for a second that I was hearing things, but then he did it again. I didn't know whether to laugh or run. But I continued stepping on his crotch in my boots, pretending that his purring was the most natural thing in the world, until my legs were sore and he was hurt enough to have an orgasm. I left the punter's car unable to believe what had just happened. I was disgusted with myself, but I was glad that I didn't have to have sex with him. I realised that it was getting late and there was no sign of Cindy, so I decided to make my way back to Ballymun.

As I walked through the mucky fields towards Cindy's flat, I noticed that all her lights were on. I couldn't wait to get inside, have a turn-on and tell her everything that had happened. She had her fair share of freaks as well, I thought to myself, as I pressed the button for the lift. The lift opened and to my absolute horror I stood face to face with Derek. 'Where d'ye think you're going?' he said calmly, looking demented.

I knew that I had to be careful what I said to him. 'I was on my way up to Cindy's. I needed somebody to talk to after the argument that we had.'

'So where have you been all this time?' he said, fists clenched with tension.

'I went for a walk to clear my head,' I said calmly. If only he knew.

Derek started to laugh. 'Do I have fuckin' eegit written on my forehead? I know exactly what you've been up to. And you needn't bother going up to Cindy's. I just smashed her door down and I really don't think she wants to see you at the moment. Now, I'll ask you again, where were you?'

I had no choice but to tell him everything. He may have frightened me earlier, but the tables had turned and now *I* was the bad one.

Derek listened to me intently, then said. 'So ye want to use, d'ye? C'mon then, let's go.' With my tail between my legs I did as he said. We both ended up taking heroin that night.

———

From then on I felt indebted to Derek. He was back using drugs. He had lost his job as a labourer and it was all my fault. But he promised me that I would never have to sell my body again. He became my partner in crime, showing me how to creep into factories and offices to steal petty-cash boxes and anything else that was worth taking. He taught me how to break into apartments and how to do smash-and-grabs. We became like Bonnie and Clyde, feeling invincible and going on robbing rampages every day. We would dress up in business suits in order to take the junkie look off of ourselves and we would brazenly fleece the shops, taking everything, from shelves of Waterford crystal to trays of jewellery. We had buyers all over Dublin and we would make sure to get rid of the stolen goods as quickly as we could. We lived for the moment and thrived on the excitement of it all. But Derek's mother started to question where all the money was coming from. When she confronted him, he went crazy and started wrecking the place. Derek's brother chased him out of the house and told him never to come back again.

Derek was beginning to show his other side. I was terrified of him, but I felt trapped. Trapped between him and the heavy brick that was my addiction. And I had no idea how to escape. We spent our nights sleeping in cars and sometimes if we were lucky we would find unoccupied apartments that were fully decorated and ready for someone to move into.

Then Derek began to sell drugs around Ballymun. He would walk around as though he owned the place, wearing his favourite red puffa jacket, with an old pair of tracksuit bottoms and slippers. People would make a joke out of his dress sense but they knew not to push him too far.

We both needed somewhere to stay in Ballymun, so Derek brought me to an empty flat that we were allowed to use for a couple of weeks. He took out our heroin and began to cook up. 'Put me out a bit, will you,' I said timidly.

'No, you're not getting any,' he said through gritted teeth.

'That's my gear as well, you know,' I protested.

He just glared at me and I knew that I was walking on eggshells. He knew that he could torture me by withholding drugs. Eventually, he said, 'Why should I when you're doin' the fuckin' dirt on me?' I knew that he was just looking for an argument, so I kept my mouth shut until he calmed down and eventually handed me the heroin. After having a turn-on I slept all day and night. When I woke up the next day I couldn't move. I hadn't eaten in days and I felt really weak. Derek told me that I had slept all that time with my eyes open and I knew that our chaotic lifestyle was wearing me down. I stayed indoors for about a week, living in squalor and keeping our drugs, munchies and cigarettes at hands reach. I felt empty and powerless, especially when Derek wanted to have sex. He would aggressively pull my head back by my hair, almost choking me. But I couldn't seem to find the energy or the courage to tell him to stop.

At this stage, I hadn't seen my family in weeks. When I did finally go home, my grandparents and Laurence were shocked to see the state that I was in. 'Oh my God, what have you done to yourself?' my grandmother shrilled. 'Go and have a shower and put your pyjamas on and I'll make you something to eat.' My grandfather was sitting like a statue in the kitchen, frozen in shock. His face dropped when he saw me. 'Holy Jaysus, what are you like!' he said and then went back to reading his newspaper. Laurence still didn't want to speak to me. 'I don't want to know. No wonder you're in a heap, with all those scumbags you hang around with. You're just as bad as them anyway,' he said as he ran up to his bedroom and stayed there for the night. I have only now come to realise just how much pain I inflicted on Laurence. At the time, no-one really said anything to me about my problems, except to make sarcastic remarks. I had grown up with a family where no-one knew how to express themselves. We kept the peace at all costs.

My Nanny told me that Mick and my mother were having difficulties in their relationship. I wasn't one bit surprised. I had witnessed for myself just how much Mick loved the women. He had never done anything in front of me, but just like my mother, I had a sneaking suspicion that he was having an affair. When my mother and Philip came to visit, I hardly spoke to her. I could barely even look at her. I blamed her for everything. For not being there for me and for not protecting me from all the bad things that had happened in my life. She had *never* been there for me. She never once sat me down and told me why she had left me with my grandparents. She never asked me why I was taking drugs. She superficially dipped in and out of my life, looking beautiful and pretending that her life was wonderful. I knew my mother wasn't happy. I knew that she was running away from me, but I had no idea why. For some reason she couldn't speak openly with me. And I couldn't help but take it personally.

My brother Philip was eleven years old and he was beginning to question why I lived with my grandparents and not with him and my mother. I told him the same thing that my grandmother had told me: it was because I had grown up in Ballymun and I didn't want to leave my school and my friends. I knew that Philip was lonely and he wanted to spend more time with me. He would follow me around everywhere in my grandparents' house, watching every movement that I made and looking for approval in everything that he did. But I could never spend time with Philip because I was too busy thinking about myself and my drug habit.

I also had very little contact at this time with my aunties Marion or Jacqueline, even though they had been like sisters to me when I was a child. Marion and her husband Declan were living in their beautiful house in Swords and were in the process of adopting a baby from Thailand. When Marion did come to visit my grandparents I would run out of the house. For some reason I felt more ashamed around Marion than I did with the rest of my family. Marion had high expectations of me as a child. She had always made a point of encouraging me to get an education. I knew that I had let her down. My other aunt, Jacqueline, had got herself a job in Dublin Airport. She was branching out on her own and trying to make a life for herself. My uncle Laurence had just broken up with his long-term girlfriend, Gail. He blamed me for this, telling me that if he hadn't put so much energy into trying to help me get clean, he would still be with Gail. Sometimes I believed him. But I knew that the real reason why he had broken up with Gail was because he had taken heavily to the alcohol. I noticed that Laurence was beginning to let his good looks go. He was losing interest in his appearance. He could barely hold down a job and he was spending most of his time in the pub. Every time I saw him he was angry. He hated me, he hated my grandfather and it seemed that he was beginning to hate himself. All that Laurence seemed to do was put me down, calling me a scumbag and telling me that I would never get clean. Maybe it was easier for him to blame all of his problems on me than to take responsibility for them himself—I should know; I'd spent most of my life doing exactly the same thing.

With my family in difficulty, I decided to go back to Derek, thinking, better the devil you know. We decided to stock up on money and drugs. We had got our hands on some stolen credit cards and after putting on our best clothes and our posh accents, we headed into a city-centre department store to do some serious shopping. It was 5.45 p.m., fifteen minutes before the shops would close. This was the best time to be scamming because the floor-walkers and security guards would be in no humour to do anything but go home. We grabbed the best of everything, from clothes to household goods, and nobody blinked an eye as we handed over the stolen credit card to pay for our items.

We were just about to leave the shop when Derek noticed a dressing-gown that he knew his mother would love. 'I have to get it,' he said.

'Just leave it, will ye. You're getting greedy,' I warned him. But he wouldn't listen. Once again he handed over the credit card. But when the cashier disappeared for more than two minutes, we knew that they were on to us. We calmly walked to the nearest blind spot where the camera couldn't see us, then we got down onto our hands and knees and we crawled our way to the nearest fire exit. 'When I count to three, I'm gonna kick the door open, so leg it,' Derek whispered. Derek kicked the door and we both ran as fast as we could down two flights of stairs. Then we burst out of the fire exit that led us onto one of the busiest streets in the city centre.

'Will you fuckin' run,' Derek shouted and pushed me at the same time. But my feet couldn't go as fast as I wanted them to and before I knew it I had fallen flat on my face. Within seconds there were two security guards running towards us. Taking me by the hand as I lay on the ground, Derek dragged me up Henry Street, but the security guards caught up with us. One of them grabbed my leg and had a tug of war with Derek. 'Just run, will you,' I shouted at Derek, preferring that one of us got away.

I was arrested, charged with fraud and, with a couple of

warrants already hanging over my head, I was put back into Mountjoy Prison.

Chapter 10 ❧

| NOTHING CHANGES

Mountjoy was stuck in a time warp, with the same people coming and going year after year. I saw so many familiar faces this time, but no matter what I did to fit in, I still stuck out like a sore thumb. I was tall, blonde and still reasonably smart-looking, in spite of having wrecked myself on drugs: to most of the girls I was a snob and some of them would call me 'Little Miss Make-up'. But I had changed a lot since my first visit, at fifteen. I was older and more street-wise. I was clever and I knew how to protect myself in prison by hanging around with girls who took no shit from anyone. I guaranteed myself safety, and prevented withdrawals, by having a regular supply of drugs and I always made sure to sort out a couple of the girls, as they did with me. And my own, from Ballymun, always looked out for me.

Derek was my life-line. Every couple of days he would smuggle me in grams of heroin. Sometimes he would put the heroin into a tennis ball and he would throw it over the prison wall, making sure that it landed in the women's yard. But this way usually caused trouble because everyone would know that I had heroin and they would be around me like flies on shite. So we decided to take the risk of him kissing it over to me when he came to visit. But there was no physical contact allowed on visits, so Derek would count to three and we would both lean over the counter. We would lock our lips together as he flicked the heroin into my mouth. The officers would grab me by the throat in an effort to stop me swallowing the drugs, but I always managed to get rid of them. They would throw me in a padded cell for a couple of hours, which gave me a chance to vomit the drugs back up. By doing this I lost my visits with Derek, so he resorted to sewing the heroin into the hem of the clothes he brought me when visiting was allowed again.

We always found a way to get drugs into Mountjoy, but getting needles and citric acid inside was much more difficult. I had always promised myself that I would never share a needle with anyone, but my habit had become much bigger and my withdrawals were more severe, so I felt I had no choice in the matter. Myself and my two friends shared our needles between us. We made sure to clean them as well as we could and sometimes we would have to burn the top of the needle to get rid of any bacteria. The needle would be like a blunt nail after a while and I found it harder to get a hit. My veins already had thrombosis from using, so when I saw how easy it was for my friend to get a hit into her groin, I asked her to do the same for me. I was terrified of using into my groin, so I covered my eyes with my hands and prayed that she wouldn't inject the heroin into an artery. I tried to distract myself from the possibility of losing a leg. But she knew exactly what she was doing and she got the vein straight away.

After one week of being held in custody, I was given a sentence of three months' imprisonment. My grandmother rang me every day and she would visit me twice every week, carrying along with her black bags full of my clothes, toiletries and new magazines. She would look like an angel, with her clear skin, her soft eyes and her curly auburn hair, never complaining and telling me over and over again that I would be grand. My mother didn't want to know. The last place she wanted to visit was Mountjoy Prison, and she was the last person I wanted a visit from.

I spent my days hanging around the cells with the other prisoners, getting tips on how to pull off a good stroke. Sometimes out of sheer boredom I would go to the prison school, just for the entertainment of watching the inmates slagging off the officers who were instructing us. Then in the evening time I would put on a tracksuit and I would go to aerobics classes. I tried my best to put on a brave face, but when the cell door closed at lock-up time and the lights were turned off, I would hide under my duvet covers and cry my heart out. How do I keep getting myself into these situations? I would ask myself in sheer frustration. Why can't I stop using drugs and just have a normal life? But I had no idea of how to live a normal life without drugs. Drugs *were* my life. And without them I had no identity.

I was released from Mountjoy Prison three days after my eighteenth birthday in October 1997 and I was taken on in a methadone clinic in Ballymun where I was given a maintenance to replace the heroin. In my mind, going on a methadone maintenance was a death sentence. At least with the heroin, if I ever really wanted to get clean it would only take a couple of weeks to go through the withdrawals. I had heard that the withdrawals from methadone were far worse. It was as though the methadone crept its way into your bones, making it nearly impossible to come off it. Most people I knew who were on maintenance had been for years and they didn't seem much healthier than on heroin. Nonetheless, I convinced the doctors that I was willing to do a maintenance, telling myself that I would just take it until after Christmas.

Myself and Derek prepared ourselves well for Christmas. We got a few bob from robbing an expensive gift shop in town. Derek had sussed the shop out well. He knew exactly what time the security guard went on his lunch break. We made sure to look the part, wearing our best suits, complete with false name tags, to make it look as if we were one of the staff. 'Be brazen, Rachael,' Derek told me as we entered the shop and walked straight over to the window display, clearing thousands of pounds worth of Waterford crystal and Lladro ornaments into our bags.

We bought enough drugs to do us until St Stephen's Day and we both decided that we would spend time with our own families.

Christmas Day arrived and I dreaded having to spend time with my family in the absolute pretence that things were just fine. I needed to get something into my body so that I could function around them. I knew that my mother and Philip would be visiting along with Jacqueline, Marion and Declan. So I hid behind my bed and had a turn-on. When I woke up I was lying on my bed and Laurence was holding me by the shoulders.

'What are ye doing?' I asked him, still in shock and feeling like I had been hit by a truck.

'Ye fuckin' overdosed, ye stupid bitch.' He was sweating, his face was red and his eyes were beginning to well up. But I couldn't remember a thing. I looked at myself in the mirror and I didn't recognise the person that looked back at me. My face appeared gaunt and I was so thin that my head looked bigger than my body. By now it just wasn't an option for me to use into my groin—I had mistakenly injected into my artery so many times that my groin felt as hard as a brick. I had resorted to injecting into my hands and I wondered how I would hide the damage that I had done to them from my family. I wanted to climb up into the attic and stay there until Christmas was over. But instead I had another turn-on. Once again, I overdosed. But this time my grandmother found me. She was screaming her head off. 'One of these days, I'll find you dead. Get dressed and come downstairs.' I did as she said.

Downstairs smelt of cinnamon with a hint of alcohol and Laurence was already half drunk. It wasn't long before the rest of my family arrived. My mother was also half drunk and I knew that she had been crying. As soon as she saw me, she put her arms around me. 'My darling daughter, I'm so sorry,' she said, holding my face in her hands.

'Sorry for what?' I was so out of it, I didn't know how to respond.

'I'm just so sorry,' she said as she began to cry.

'Now, Lynda, don't start,' my grandmother interrupted, but my mother continued, 'Oh my God, look at your hands. What have you done to yourself. I'm so sorry,' she said taking me into her arms.

'C'mon now, Lynda, you're talking rubbish,' Nanny insisted.

'I'm not talking rubbish, Mam. I'm grand.' My mother sat beside me holding my hand in hers and I wished that she could be this affectionate with me when she was sober. Was she really as sorry as she said she was, or was it just the drink talking?

We all had Christmas dinner together except for Laurence. He sat in the sitting-room with my uncle Declan, as far away as possible from me. My grandmother watched me like a hawk, making sure that I didn't sneak off to use heroin. I knew that I would get my chance when Laurence's friends came over later on that night. They were having a party and I would have to wait patiently until everybody was too drunk to even notice that I was gone. Eventually my time came and I was left alone. Everyone was in the sitting-room but it wouldn't be long before my grandmother came back into the kitchen. So as quickly as I could I got my heroin into my needle and I tried to inject it into my hand. But I couldn't get a vein. I badly needed to get a hit so I stood in front of the mirror and, holding my nose and keeping my mouth shut, I blew as hard as I could until I saw a vein appear in the front of my neck. I got the vein straight away and within seconds I could feel a warm overwhelming rush travel from my toes up into my head. I knew that I was going to overdose so I tried to get outside to get some air. But before I made it to the door, I collapsed.

When I opened my eyes I was faced with two ambulance men. 'Don't get up. Just stay where you are,' one of them warned me. Then I saw my family and Laurence's friends. They were just staring at me as I lay on the floor. Then I realised what had happened and the first thing I thought of was my supply of heroin. 'Me gear, where's me gear?' I screamed, starting to panic.

'Don't move, Rachael,' said the ambulance man as he held me down by the arm.

'No. Stop! I'm ok. I need to find my gear.'

'We need to bring you into the hospital to make sure that you're ok.'

'No, I'm not going to the hospital. Look I'm alright,' I told them as I struggled to stand up. I was still seeing double but I pretended that I was fine.

The ambulance men stayed with me until I was well enough to walk around on my own. As soon as they were gone, I searched everywhere for my heroin. 'I have to find my gear. One of you took it, didn't you? You'd better give it back to me. I need it,' I shouted at my family, as I ran around the house like a mad woman. Then I put my hand into my pocket and there was my bag of heroin. 'Oh, look, I found it. It was in my pocket,' I told my family and everyone else that was in the house. They just turned their faces in disgust. But in that moment I didn't care what anyone thought. Once I had my heroin everything would be ok.

———

It had been the worst Christmas ever and I couldn't bear to be near my family, so myself and Derek found a flat that we could squat in on the south side of Dublin. We spent months in the flat, locked into our own world of numbness and squalor and the only time we had contact with the outside world was when we had to go off robbing, or we needed to score some heroin.

When we were asked to sell heroin for a big-time drug-dealer we willingly agreed—we knew that we could get somebody else to sell it for us and that way we could keep our heads down and keep our habits going at the same time. Every couple of days the dealer would drop the heroin in through our window. We would bag it up and a friend of ours would sell it for us. Any profit that was made, we injected into our bodies. But it wasn't long before we became our own best customers and began to build up a debt to the drug dealer. AJ was his name. He looked like an elegant businessman, who wore immaculate designer suits and had a manicure done almost every week. But I knew by him that he would be very capable of cutting either one of us up in a split second. AJ was a control freak who got great pleasure out of playing games with myself and Derek. When we told him that we hadn't got his money, he wasn't pleased and he asked us to meet up with him.

AJ arrived at the meeting place wearing a knee-length Versace coat with his hair combed perfectly to the side. He invited us both into his car and he asked Derek to drive. We told him that we would make it up to him and we would get his money as soon as possible. AJ was wired to the moon on cocaine and my heart skipped a beat when he pulled out a knife. He put his finger up to his mouth signalling for me to be quiet. Then he put the knife to the nape of Derek's neck. 'Don't turn around, Derek. D'you realise I could knife you right now and you wouldn't be able to do a thing.'

For a moment everything went silent. Then suddenly AJ burst out laughing. 'I'm only buzzing off you, you mad thing,' he said. 'But ye better get me that money.' AJ left us on the side of the road and drove off, still laughing to himself. It was the first time that I had ever seen Derek bow down or be afraid of someone. Within a couple of days we had managed to get AJ's money, and we decided to give him a wide berth from then on. But we still needed drugs, so we had no choice but to go back to robbing.

My body now felt as though it was giving in. I couldn't cope any more with my life being so unpredictable. I couldn't cope with the withdrawals that I felt every morning from using heroin, the aching pains in my legs and my stomach and butchering myself until I got a vein. Things had got so bad that Derek couldn't get out of the bed to use the toilet, so he would urinate into a bottle instead. We lived like animals and I wondered when it would all end. We were both caught in a spiral, urging each other on to use, completely dependent on each other to keep the vicious cycle going, neither of us able to break it.

At this time, one of Derek's friends, Paul, had been released from prison. He had nowhere to stay so Derek told him that he could come and stay with us. I had no say in the matter. An addict himself, Paul needed to make some quick money and, after myself and Derek had sussed out a factory to rob, I let Paul do it on condition that he sort me out with some heroin. So they both went off robbing and when they came back they had enough money and heroin to do us for a few days. They got down to business straight away, putting their heroin out on the spoons. 'Will I give ye some gear now, Rachael?' asked Paul.

'No, don't give her anything,' Derek shouted.

'Don't mind him, Paul, you know the deal,' I said.

Then Derek picked up a bowl and he flung it across the room. 'You're not getting any 'cos you're only a fuckin' slut.'

'Ah, here we go again. What are you talking about now?' I said.

'I heard that you were with someone out in Ballymun that had the virus.'

'Oh my God,' I screamed, 'how could I be with someone else when I'm with you twenty-four hours a day?' Derek had been becoming increasingly paranoid about me and other men and had been keeping a very close eye on me.

Sensing that the situation was about to turn ugly, Paul quickly had a turn-on and then told us that he was leaving. 'No, don't go, Paul. Don't leave me on my own with him,' I pleaded. But Paul went anyway. Alone with a paranoid Derek, I began to cry hysterically.

'Shut up fuckin' cryin',' Derek demanded. He came over to me and helped me onto the chair. 'Just stop cryin', will ye?' he said. He disappeared for a moment and when he came back he had planks of wood and a hammer in his hands. I watched him in disbelief as he proceeded to nail the planks of wood onto the door, humming a tune to himself as he did so. I sat with my knees to my chest, hyperventilating and crippled with fear. 'Now you won't be going anywhere, will you?' he said. I assumed that he had lost the plot altogether.

I needed to get out of the flat, and quick, but Derek had taken my phone so that I couldn't make contact with anybody. But the next day when he wasn't looking I managed to get my hands on my phone. I sent my grandmother a message telling her to send Laurence to the flat as quickly as she could. Within a couple of hours I could hear my grandmother's voice outside the door. She was with my mother and they banged on the door until Derek had no choice but to let them inside. As soon as Derek saw my mother, his demeanour completely changed. He rapidly went from being a monster to being a little mouse.

My mother went berserk when she saw what he had done. 'You won't get away with this, you fuckin' pig,' she screamed at him as they took me out of the flat. My grandmother brought me back to her house so that she could look after me. I had no methadone or heroin and I felt battered, bruised and spiritually broken. Not only from Derek, but also from the drugs. I was never so grateful to be back in my own bed. I could breathe freely without worrying about what was going to happen next. Laurence and my grandfather knew that I had been through a tough time, so for once they kept their mouths closed and left me alone.

For five days I went through my withdrawals, feeling as though I had worms in my legs that were aggressively eating away at my bones. But the worst part was my mind. It was twisting and turning, trying to make sense of my life. I didn't have the capacity to see past my own hand. I had no mental defence for my addiction, or any knowledge of how to escape from it. People had told me that I would stop using drugs when I had hit rock bottom. If this wasn't rock bottom, then I didn't know what was. Things couldn't possibly get any worse. I was so desperate that suicide seemed the only way out.

Later on that morning the gardaí came to my grandparents'

house and arrested me on outstanding warrants for theft. Once again I was sent to Mountjoy and in a strange way I was relieved. Even after all that had happened, I wasn't sure if I would have the strength to stay away from Derek and the gear. I had a feeling that going to Mountjoy would be a blessing in disguise.

Chapter 11 ℘

| ANSWERED PRAYERS

They say that things have to get worse before they get better and that was certainly the case for me. I had reached a new low in my addiction and was facing another stint in Mountjoy, after which I would be released and the whole cycle would begin again. I needed help, but didn't know where to look for it. I've never been a spiritual person and it never occurred to me to seek help from that direction. But that is exactly the place from where help came, just when I most needed it.

After one week in custody I was brought to court to face my warrants and I had no doubt in my mind that I would be given a hefty sentence. The Dublin District Court was full of activity, with solicitors and gardaí buzzing up and down from the courtroom to the holding cells. The holding cells were bursting at the seams with prisoners awaiting sentences.

After being informed by my solicitor that I could get a sentence of anything up to two years for each charge, as I had previous convictions, I resigned myself to the fact that I was getting locked up. Then I heard somebody mention my name. I looked outside of the holding cell and I saw a priest. 'Here I am,' I shouted to him, confused as to why the priest was looking for me and feeling like I was seeing an apparition.

'Hi, Rachael, my name is Father Adrian,' the priest said gently. 'I know we've never met before, but a nurse in Beaumont Hospital gave me your mother's number. She said that you were very sick and that you needed help to overcome your addiction.'

Father Adrian was exactly what I expected a priest to be like. He was a beacon of light and full of humility and I felt immediately reassured by his presence. 'I got in touch with your mother and she brought me here to see you,' he continued. I still couldn't comprehend what was going on and I was conscious of the other prisoners sitting behind me, trying to hear what Father Adrian was saying.

'Now, have you ever heard of a place called Community Cenacolo?' I shook my head. 'It's a community in Italy run by a nun called Sister Elvira. She is an amazing woman and she has helped thousands of people to get clean. Would you be interested in going over?'

'Emm, I really don't think I'll be going anywhere today, Father,' I replied. 'I have a load of charges and I'm just about to get sentenced.'

'Don't worry. I'll do my best and I'll try to sort something out.'

'I'll go to Italy with ye, Father,' shouted one of the girls sitting beside me. Father Adrian just smiled and he was gone. I began to wonder if I had dreamed him up.

———

Just before my name was called to stand in front of the judge, my old friend Garda PJ Walsh from Ballymun came marching over to me. 'Who's this priest?' he said.

'He's a friend of the family,' I told him.

'Right, are you willing to go to Italy?'

'Yeah, if the judge gives me bail.'

'But you're already serving a sentence.'

'I know. I'll put in for temporary release.'

'This is what I'll do then,' said PJ. 'I won't object to bail and I won't say anything about you serving a sentence, but I'm fuckin' warning you, if you fuck up one more time I'll personally give you a good hidin' myself. D'you understand?' said PJ as he jokingly showed me his fist. But I knew that he was deadly serious about me messing up.

'Yeah, thanks, PJ,' I humbly agreed.

PJ was as good as his word. He stood in the witness box and he never objected to bail. He told the judge that I came from a good family whom he had known for the past eight years. I was a young girl who had gotten mixed up with the wrong crowd, he said. He had witnessed my addiction spiral out of control and he thought that my life depended on me going to Italy.

I couldn't believe my ears. But when I thought about it, PJ always did have a soft spot for me. When he was finished in the witness box, it was Father Adrian's turn. He told the judge all about the community and how strict it was and about how it was my only hope.

But the judge wasn't having any of it. 'This girl stands before me with a list of charges and outstanding warrants and she has also been sent forward to the circuit court for burglary of a phone shop. Give me one good reason why I should send her on a tour around Italy. No, no, no. She's not going and that's it. Put her back into custody and I will deal with her tomorrow,' demanded the judge.

And this is how things went for three days. I went from custody to court as everyone fought for me to be released. The judge was adamant that I not go to Italy. I had been given too many chances already, he said. But my solicitor wouldn't give in. She told him that this would be my last chance; if I didn't go to Italy now, I would never get clean from drugs. She assured him that he would receive monthly reports on my progress. In the end the judge reluctantly agreed. He put tight bail conditions on me that depended on my staying in the community for one year.

———

It was Friday afternoon and I wasn't out of the woods yet. I had my charges out of the way, but now I had to apply for temporary release from Mountjoy Prison. My mother and my grandmother had, in blind faith, booked me onto a flight to Italy for eight o'clock on the Saturday morning. As soon as I got back to Mountjoy Prison I put my application form in for temporary release. The hours passed and I paced my cell hoping that things would go according to plan. But nine o'clock came and went and I was certain that I was going nowhere. After asking the officers if they had heard anything about me being released, they told me that it was too late. My heart sank. Fuck it anyway, I thought. I had got my hopes up for nothing. It would be impossible to get clean in prison and there was no chance of me getting clean on the outside.

I spent the rest of the night with the other prisoners, many of whom I knew from Ballymun, reminiscing about the good old days when we went to raves and before the heroin had us in its grip. And for a split second I felt as though I could see myself from outside my body. I no longer stood out like a sore thumb: I was just like all the other prisoners upon whom I had once looked down my nose. I looked like them and I acted like them. I had lost all my pride and my inhibitions. I had become a horrible, selfish person who abused my family and any friends I had. And for the first time in my life I could clearly see just how sick I was.

That night I prayed to God, begging him to help me. 'Please God, give me one more chance. I promise I'll do my best this time.' I drifted off to sleep and as usual I dreaded what the next day would bring.

Looking back now, I may have been at rock bottom with my addiction and about to face a lengthy spell in Mountjoy, but I'm not really sure that I was ready to give up drugs. I now know what being truly 'ready' is: deciding of my own will that I wanted a life free from drugs, that there was a life beyond heroin. Then, I was simply desperate for a way out of the degradation of prostitution and thieving and the wreckage of my life. And it looked as if my prayers had been answered.

———

My cell door opened the next morning. 'C'mon, Rachael, it's your lucky day. You're getting TR,' shouted one of the officers.

'What? How come? What time is it?' I said, hopping out of my bed, still half asleep and convinced that they were making a mistake.

The officer explained, 'Your mother put a block on you being released before now. Herself and your grandmother are outside waiting for you, so hurry up.' My mother had obviously been afraid that if I had been released earlier, I would just have made a run for it back to my old life. Perhaps she was right. I grabbed my belongings as quickly as I could before the officers found a reason to keep me locked up.

As I hurried out of the prison I could hear the other prisoners shouting across to one another. 'Here, Elaine, are ye listenin'? D'ye ever see the fuckin' likes of it? Getting TR at four o'clock in the fuckin' morning! Ye'd wanna be a fuckin' rat to pull that one.' But I couldn't care less what the other prisoners thought of me. My prayers had been answered. I was taking this opportunity with both hands and making the best of it.

———

I was so sick after my flight and the withdrawals that I hardly knew what was going on. I found it strange that my mother had come with me—usually she would get somebody else to do her dirty work, like Laurence or Mick. I watched her carefully, trying to figure out what her motive was. Had she finally realised how much I needed her to be my mother, or was she just trying to get rid of me again? Either way, I didn't care. Like a child I was just happy that she was with me, regardless of her reasons.

Father Adrian gave us directions to meet the people from the community in a little hostel in Turin. Two men arrived late on Saturday night wearing military jackets and looking like they weren't to be messed with. I said my goodbyes to my mother and my grandmother as they handed me into the care of these strange men. I had no idea of what I was getting myself into, but nothing could be worse than where I was coming from.

I had fallen asleep on our way to the community and when I woke up I could feel my withdrawals kicking in. This was the part that I dreaded the most. For me, the withdrawals were what I lived in fear of every day: I had never left myself long enough without heroin to feel the severity of going cold turkey. I wouldn't rest until I had enough drugs to keep the sickness at bay. I had taken ninety mls of methadone before I left Mountjoy: it was still in my system and keeping me going but the dope sickness had started and the rest was in the post.

I was informed that I was being taken to a house called Savliganno. When we arrived I was greeted with a firm handshake by my appointed guardian angel, Dubrilla. She appeared to be in her early forties, with shoulder-length grey hair and tanned skin. I guessed she was eastern European. With Dubrilla there was no beating around the bush. 'You are very welcome to the community, but don't for one minute expect it to be easy,' she said. 'All of your belongings will be taken from you and you won't get them back until the time is right.' She approached me with a cup of tea. 'Drink it. It will help you sleep. You will realise yourself that in Community Cenacolo there is a reason for everything. Now it's late, so you should try and get some rest.'

Less of the fuckin' attitude, I wanted to say to her, still with the prison chip on my shoulder. But I used my head and I did as she said.

I felt as though I had only closed my eyes and opened them again when I saw Dubrilla standing by my bunk bed. She was staring at me. 'I thought you were dead. You have mascara all over you,' she said while she touched my face.

Ah, fuck off away from me, I thought, wanting to throw a tantrum. 'It's too early, Dubrilla,' I said.

'You have already slept over by three hours. It's nine o'clock and you have to get up.'

'I can't move, Dubrilla. I'm in bits,' I protested.

'I know, but if you lie in bed you will feel worse. Look how beautiful the day is,' she said as she opened the blinds. 'I want to show you something.'

I dragged myself out of the bed and I went to where she stood. '*Bellissimo,* eh?' she said, pointing to the view. We were surrounded by the Alpine mountains and the sun blistered down onto layers of golden cornfields. 'We have our own greenhouse and we grow our own vegetables,' she enthused. I had more interest in the man on the moon than in her little pep talk. I just wanted to jump back into bed, close my eyes and never wake up.

'Oh look! There are the girls going for their walk,' she said. I followed her pointing finger and saw at least twenty women walking in a perfect line of twos. 'They're walking the rosary,' she said.

'Come again?! What do you mean, "Walking the rosary?"'

'Every Sunday we go for a walk and say the rosary. And now that Lent is coming, we will be doing it a lot more. It's really nice,' she said, staring at the girls with a smile on her face.

'Why are they in twos?'

'Because Jesus always sent his disciples out in twos.'

Ah, this is just fuckin' great, I thought. I've just walked myself into a mad cult. I had heard of places like Community Cenacolo, where everyone spoke in tongues and prayed over vulnerable addicts, putting the fear of God into them and brain-washing them. As if reading my mind, Dubrilla grinned, 'Don't worry, we won't force you into doing anything. I'm sure that you will do it when you are ready. But it will be expected of you to work, just like everybody else. For the first week, while you are sick, you will work with me in the factory. We make car parts,' she said. 'Then you will work in the garden. The fresh air will make you stronger. So let's go! I will give you some clothes.'

Dubrilla handed me a pile of old clothes. 'I know it's not easy when you're stripped of all your material goods,' she said. This was unbearable. It was one thing going through my sickness, but expecting me to wear long flowing skirts with Jesus sandals and no make-up was just torture. 'Just trust me,' she said.

When the other girls returned from their walk, Dubrilla introduced me to them all. Most of them were either Italian or Croatian and they couldn't speak a word of English. Thank God, I thought, at least they won't be able to preach to me about the Bible or anything. And there was no way these girls were addicts: they all looked so healthy and happy. But as weak as I was, I was struck by their simplicity. I was curious about the glow that they had in their eyes.

I tried my best to be friendly, but my sickness was getting worse. My insides felt as though they were about to empty out of me and my joints were drying up and needed to be oiled. Dubrilla stayed by my side until six o'clock came. She told me that it was 'junkie talk time' in the chapel. I had visions of people levitating and collapsing mid-prayer. I was intrigued and I didn't want to miss out on anything, so I went along with them. Everyone sat in a circle and spoke about how her day had gone. I didn't understand what they were saying, but in Italian it sounded good. Then the girls knelt down and said a rosary. I had come directly from prison to this. I was way out of my comfort zone. But I joined them out of respect.

After the chapel it was dinner time. The smell of the food was making me heave. I couldn't leave Dubrilla's side until it was time to go to bed. I knew that I wouldn't sleep, but when the time came

I was relieved to get away from everyone. I lay in my bed staring into the darkness, frozen with fear. I really wanted to get clean, but I didn't want to become a holy Joe. Nobody would want to know me then, I thought, but then, no-one wants to know me anyway. Sure I don't even deserve to be on this planet after all the bad things I've done. And my family had seen that a long time ago. 'You're nothing but a scum-bag,' I told myself. 'You're better off dead.' I remembered myself as that little girl in Temple Street hospital, every Sunday in the chapel with the nuns, singing away to my heart's content, oblivious to what lay ahead. I pushed back the tears. If God loved me that much, why did he fuck off on me like that? Why hadn't he helped me a long time ago? 'Because you don't deserve God's love, that's why?' I answered myself.

My head wouldn't stop racing and I felt as though I were being suffocated by a cloak of negativity. Eventually I got some sleep, but when I woke up it was still dark outside. I was lying in a pool of sweat and my hands were swollen from clenching my fists so tightly. It was time to get up. I was told to get washed and dressed in my work clothes and to be in the chapel as quickly as possible. We started the day with the Joyful Mysteries. But I was far from joyful and in no humour to go to work. The day dragged on as myself and some other girls worked in an assembly line. I desperately tried to distract myself from how shit I felt by talking to Dubrilla. She told me the story of Sister Elvira, who had founded the community, and of the revelation that had come to her to help hopeless drug-addicts and how she had transformed people's lives the world over.

Still I couldn't stop thinking of drugs. I kept making excuses to go to the toilet, just to get away from Dubrilla, but she trailed behind me everywhere I went. I was craving everything: drugs, a cigarette, my clothes and my make-up—anything to make me feel a bit better. However, I had no choice but to persevere. By the time I got to bed that night I was physically and mentally exhausted, but my mind still wouldn't slow down. I wonder if blind people dream? And if they do can they see in their dreams? My mind rambled around and around. 'Oh, shut up!' I argued with myself. I wanted to chop my head and my legs off so that I wouldn't feel the pain.

Before I knew it, it was morning time again. Dubrilla came to my bed, bright-eyed and bushy tailed, and I just wanted to hit her. 'Don't even ask me to get up, 'cos I can't move,' I growled at her, my hair stuck to my head.

'You can stay in bed for two more hours, but you're being put in the garden today,' she replied.

Before I knew it I was sitting in a field with a pair of scissors in my hand. 'What are the scissors for, Dubrilla?'

'For cutting the grass.'

'Ha, ha, very funny.'

'No, really, I'm telling you the truth.'

'Why can't I use the lawn-mower over there?' I said.

'Because this will help you to grow in patience,' she replied, smiling.

I was being pushed to my limits and I felt like stabbing myself or Dubrilla with the scissors. The hours passed by with me cutting the grass, trapped in my head. It was scorching outside but I was shivering with the cold. My nose was running, I couldn't stop yawning and my back was aching, all symptoms of withdrawal.

'You're not allowed to kneel down,' said Dubrilla, as I tried to get comfortable on the grass. 'You have to kneel up.'

Oh will you just get out of my face; you probably don't even know what drugs look like, I told her in my head. I couldn't see Dubrilla, or even the grass that I was cutting. All I could see were my thoughts, whizzing past me like a movie on fast-forward. 'Ah, I can't do this, Dubrilla. I want to go home,' I wailed.

She didn't look surprised. 'Umm, why do you want to go home?'

'Because I miss my family.' She looked like she was going to laugh.

'What's so funny?'

'I suppose you have a really good relationship with your family, do you?'

'I do, yeah,' I lied.

'So why did your family leave you here then?' she probed.

'Because I have a drug problem,' I told her, feeling irritated.

'And you don't have a drug problem any more, do you not? You don't miss your family, Rachael, you miss the drugs.'

Fuckin' bitch, I said to myself, as I started to cut the grass again. The last thing I wanted to hear was the truth.

'You are on your third day now, Rachael. Two more days and the worst will be over.'

'Yeah! thanks.'

———

Even though Dubrilla drove me mad, I dreaded night-time and being left alone with my demons. My mind would spin, a dizzy mixture of self-analysis and random rubbish: What's it all about? Why are we really here? Why is bread called bread? And who thought of that word? Bread, bread, bread… I couldn't shut the thoughts off. The taste of heroin in the back of my throat was taking my breath away, and no matter what way I lay I couldn't get comfortable. It would have been better if somebody had skinned me alive and poured vinegar all over me. At least that way it would be over and done with. The muscle spasms and agitation dragged on and on, getting worse by the hour. I was endlessly heaving, but nothing would come out of my stomach except green bile.

It was still the middle of the night but I could hear commotion coming from the other dormitories. Dubrilla entered my room. 'Rachael, you have to get up. It's adoration time.'

I had no energy to get up, but I was glad of the distraction. My legs felt like a ton of bricks, but I dragged them down to the chapel along with the other girls. The chapel was small and simple, with oak wooden floors, an altar and an open eucharist. The candles created an ambience and I could barely see the other girls as they knelt down in front of me. 'Oh blood and water, which gushed forth from the heart of Jesus as a fount of mercy for us, I trust in you,' they chanted over and over again.

I don't trust in you. I'm glad you died on the cross, I thought bitterly, before correcting myself. Oh my God, how could I think such a thing? That just proves that I'm evil. Only evil people could think such things. No, I didn't mean it. God, please forgive me. I began to join the girls in their chant. I tried to visualise Jesus sitting before me, just as he was in the picture that my grandmother had of him at home. He was smiling at me, with rays of blue and red light coming from his heart, shining directly into mine. My head was beginning to slow down. I could feel the chanting break through my walls of fear and anger, until I felt raw inside. Then adoration was over, but I couldn't get up. I told Dubrilla that I needed to be left alone. I waited until everyone was gone and in the silence I cried my heart out, crumbling to pieces before the eucharist.

———

The next morning, after getting a couple of hours sleep, it was as though a weight had been lifted from my shoulders. I got dressed and headed downstairs to the kitchen. I passed the conservatory and suddenly I came to a halt. It was the first time in years that I had seen a sunrise. I hurried outside to get a proper look. The sky was cerise pink with swirls of lavender, and as I felt the warmth of the sun on my face my spirit seemed to come alive. I was still very weak, but I hadn't felt this good since I was a child. Something was shifting within me, I could feel it. I wasn't sure if it was down to the adoration or the good cry that I'd had that morning, but whatever it was, I was holding onto it. I made a decision there and then to give Community Cenacolo my best shot.

From then on, life got easier for me in the community. Adjusting to the monotony of routine was the hardest and at times I missed the excitement of my old life. But my old life still haunted me in my dreams. At times I would wake up in a panic, convinced that I had used heroin and relapsed. Or I would be left feeling disturbed by dreams of having sex with monsters, spending the rest of the day riddled with guilt and repeatedly questioning my morality. My body and my mind felt distorted and sensitive and the smallest of things would trigger off a craving for drugs.

I was eventually given back my clothes and I now understood why they were taken from me in the first place. They reminded me of my drug use. They brought me back to the person that I was on the streets of Ballymun. I couldn't stand that person inside of me. I wanted her to go away, so I decided to change my image by cutting my hair into a short shaggy bob and I was ready to embrace the holy Joe look with open arms.

Working in the garden was making me stronger in all senses. My mind was clearer from the good weather and the fresh air. My appetite was slowly coming back and I was beginning to gain some weight. The prayer and meditation seemed to stabilise me emotionally, restoring my faith in God. And for the first time in my life, I felt as though I belonged somewhere.

My tolerance of the community was put to the test during Lent: forty days and forty nights of adoration at all hours of the night. Renunciation of chocolate, coffee and anything of pleasure. I was eating, breathing and sleeping the mysteries of the rosary. And after three months I had had enough. I had found the solution to my addiction. It was God. Once I prayed every day and practised everything that I had learned from the community, then I would be sorted. I wanted out of the community.

Dubrilla and the other girls didn't agree with me. 'You need at least a year or two before you can even think of going home,' they said. They gathered around me in the office, saying everything that they could think of to try and persuade me to stay. They even rang Father Adrian and asked him to talk me out of it.

'Rachael, you can't come home. As soon as you set foot in Dublin, you will be arrested,' he said.

'Not if I stay clean,' I told him.

'Rachael, yourself and Derek were on *CrimeCall* recently. You were both seen robbing a jeweller's. The gardaí are just waiting for you to mess up.' I knew Father Adrian was telling the truth. If I was on television, I would definitely be arrested, but I convinced myself that once I stayed clean, no judge in their right mind would lock me up. I made my decision to go home.

But my mother wasn't making things easy for me. She refused to send me over a flight ticket. If I wanted to come home I would have to find my own way back, she said. I wasn't going to let her get the better of me. So without letting the girls know, I took my English-Italian pocket translator and my set of rosary beads and off I headed to the nearest Irish Embassy.

I got half-way through the cornfields when I realised what I had just done. 'Fuckin' hell, what am I at?' It was the type of thing that I would have done when I was using drugs. Acting on impulse and never thinking of the consequences. I was in a strange country with no money, no passport and nowhere to turn. But I couldn't go back now. My pride wouldn't allow me to. I would have to keep going and just hope for the best.

It was beginning to get dark and I was becoming more and more fearful that something awful might happen to me. I could see a town in the near distance and I decided to knock into the first house that I came to. The front door opened and I was shocked to be met by the local priest who took confessions from us every Sunday. I had no choice but to tell him the truth. He wasn't one bit impressed and without any delay he drove me straight back to the community. I felt humiliated when I saw the girls waiting for me in the yard. 'Don't worry. You made your point. You're going home,' said Dubrilla. She was disappointed in me and that was the last time we spoke.

Chapter 12 ∾

| ## BACK TO SQUARE ONE

'Lord Jesus, create in me an intolerance for alcohol and drugs that will prevent me from ever offending those who love me,' I prayed over and over again, as I landed in Dublin airport. I couldn't afford to mess up this time. There was no sign of any gardaí and I began to wonder if Father Adrian had been telling porkies about me being on *CrimeCall*.

My grandmother welcomed me back into her home and she was happy to see me back in full health. The rest of my family, however, were not entirely convinced that I would stay clean. They knew that being back in Ballymun so soon was dangerous for me. All I had to do was walk out my front door and heroin was there. But at the time I couldn't see myself anywhere else. The pull of the past was too strong.

By now my mother had split up with Mick. She had found out that he had been living a double life. He had been in another relationship for years without anybody knowing. When the truth came out, she was devastated to say the least. The life that she had built up for herself and Philip came tumbling down around her. In a short amount of time she lost almost everything. The house they had lived in on the southside was taken from under her feet, along with many of her material possessions. The break-up left her shattered and bitter towards everyone.

Myself and my mother were like strangers to each other at this stage. I knew about the break-up only because my grandmother had told me. Sometimes I would see her in my grandmother's house, but our conversations were light and of very little meaning. I also knew that she had taken heavily to the drink. It was frustrating to know these things about my mother and to have such a big wall between us. We were both beyond each other's reach, living in separate worlds. And for now there was nothing that we could do about it.

So, she made the decision to do what she had done best all of her life. She ran. She packed a bag and she moved over to America to live with my uncle Jonathon and his girlfriend, Jennifer. And in a way I was happy to see her go. She had nothing to keep her in Ireland. Philip was fifteen years old and he had decided to stay with his father. Everyone knew that my mother was on a slippery slope and that staying with Jonathon was the best thing for her.

My grandmother urged me to get myself a job. 'It will keep you sane,' she told me. One of my friends, Antoinette, got me a job in a taxi company. Two years older than me, she had sometimes dabbled with taking heroin, but Antoinette knew of my own battle with drugs and she promised me that she would never even mention the word 'heroin' in my presence.

Getting a job and going out into the real world completely drug-free was a big step forward for me, but my vocabulary was limited to drugs and religion and I had no idea of how to communicate with normal people. So I stuck close to Antoinette and it wasn't long before we were good friends. For the next couple of months I stayed clean, abiding by my plan of prayer and work, but my resistance to the drugs was wearing thin. This was hardly surprising: after all, I was back in Ballymun, where my associations with drugs were everywhere and I had fooled myself into thinking that I was strong enough to hang around with Antoinette and other old friends who were using drugs. It would only be a matter of time before I had a needle in my arm again. By now I was under no illusion that I could control my drug use. I was managing to keep it at bay, but I knew that it would only be a matter of time before I was back to square one.

The frustration that I felt towards myself when I came back from Italy, and all the work I had done there and ended up back on drugs, was indescribable. And it all happened so quickly. I had convinced myself that I was strong enough to help my friend Antoinette and to stay clear of drugs. My heart had been in the right place, but all along I had been unconsciously setting myself up to use again. I was right back where I had left off.

As I lay in my cell in the Bridewell garda station after being nicked for shop-lifting, I tried to get my head around how stupid I had been. What the hell is wrong with me? I screamed at myself for the millionth time. Why can't I think before I act? Why do I keep ending up in these fucking situations? God, I'm so sorry. I'll do anything, just please don't let me get locked up again.

I knew that if I came before the judge who had, reluctantly, allowed me to go to Italy, he would lock me up straight away. I found out that Derek was still in prison since I'd been in Italy. He had taken the rap for all our charges. Even the one that was on *CrimeCall.* Father Adrian had been telling the truth all along. I dreaded seeing Derek again.

Thankfully, that day none of my previous charges was mentioned in court and my new charge was put back until another date. I was free to go for now. I was more than relieved. I made my way back to my grandmother's house. My grandfather went mad when he saw me. He knew that I was back on drugs and he gave me a right earful, calling me all sorts of names.

How many times had I been in this position before? That first drug always left me a wreck, and once I used once, nothing could stop me. But my habit wasn't in full swing yet and I knew that I had to do something very quickly before I got strung out. I decided to ring my old friend, Big Mick. He had recently bought himself a new house in the country. And if anybody could help me, he was that person. After helping me that time in the Rutland and taking me to Texas, Big Mick had kept in touch with me. He took a genuine interest in me and had always supported me as best he could. After telling Big Mick everything that had happened, he agreed to let me go through cold turkey in his place. The agreement was that I would stay with him for two weeks and we would take things from there.

But two weeks turned into months and I ended up staying with him for two years. Big Mick was a character who had an amazing ability to make everyone around him laugh, but he had had his fair share of difficulties in his life. He had been a chronic drug user for a long time, but with the help of Narcotics Anonymous he had managed to get clean and get a good life for himself. He knew that in order to stay clean he had to give back to people what had been given to him. He had a big heart and he went out of his way to help others, never losing his sense of humour and always seeing the funny side of things. We spent the first few months of my stay in the country laughing our heads off and amusing ourselves by slagging all the culchies.

My experience in Community Cenacolo had taught me that the only time I felt truly fulfilled was when I prayed. I was terrified now of having a relapse, so I frantically prayed morning, noon and night. Big Mick had also been encouraged in his recovery to make contact with a power greater than himself, but it was something that he could never succumb to and he laughed it off as though it didn't apply to somebody like him. He watched my transformation in amazement and he began to question me about prayer and meditation. We would sit for hours philosophising about spirituality and life.

It was during this time that myself and Big Mick became really close. I was beginning to have feelings towards him. I was sure *he* could give me everything that I needed: love, security, happiness and fun. He had been clean for ten years now and maybe he could teach me how to live my life without drugs. I was shocked when I began to realise that Big Mick was falling for me as well. I wondered what my family would think about all this. Mick was double my age, forty-two years old. I had never before looked at

Big Mick in the light of being my lover. What was a lover anyway? I had no idea. Steo had been my first love. All the others were a necessity to keep my drug habit going, or a drug-fuelled mistake, so, in many ways, I felt that being with Big Mick would be my first real relationship.

At first we took things very slowly and we kept our relationship quiet. Mick treated me like gold, looking after me as best as he could, protecting me from myself and my addiction. At first I was living on a pink cloud. I was finally free from drugs and Mick was teaching me how to cope with my life drug-free. But before long everything came crashing down around me.

The prayer was becoming like another addiction. I couldn't function without it. It was my great escape. The heavy meditation was bringing me deeper and deeper into myself, leaving me crippled with fear and paranoia. But without the prayer I was convinced that I would relapse.

Mick was beginning to worry about my mental health. He encouraged me to get a job and to get out more. I took his advice and I forced myself to get a job in a nursing home. I was working with patients who had Alzheimer's and I found this work really rewarding. For the first time in my life I felt that I was doing something good with myself and was finally part of society. But something still wasn't right. I was an emotional wreck and I quickly realised that I was incapable of looking after myself, let alone Alzheimer's patients. Life without drugs seemed unbearable. Now that I no longer had drugs to muffle the pain, I had no control over my mind and my emotions. Memories of my past seemed to overwhelm me and I was convinced that anyone with whom I came into contact knew that I had been a drug addict. They knew exactly what I was thinking and how I was feeling, I knew. I was completely transparent and defenceless. I desperately tried to combat my negative thoughts with prayer, but the more I forced myself to feel better, the quicker I slipped into a state of depression. I was having a nervous breakdown. My doctor prescribed me anti-depressants, which seemed to give me some stability for a couple of months, but then came the extreme mood swings and panic attacks. After six months of living in the country I became phobic about leaving the house. If people saw the state I was in, they would have had me committed.

Big Mick tried everything in his power to help me: bringing me for acupuncture, counselling, art therapy and visits to Lough Derg, where I ran around barefoot with my rosary beads in a frenzied attempt to wash away my negative thoughts. But nothing seemed to work. Staying clean seemed more difficult than using drugs. I couldn't live my life like this. I was fucked up on drugs *and* off them. At least when I was using drugs I was oblivious to my defects, I thought to myself.

And then the idea took hold. Maybe now that I was living a quiet life in the country with Mick, the odd turn-on of heroin would be ok. No-one would have to know. Instead of going to work, I could sneak up to Dublin, score some gear and be back before Mick had any suspicions. I eventually came to the conclusion that I just had to use. I had no choice any more. Sure I was going to use heroin at some stage anyway, so I may as well stop tormenting myself and just do it now.

The journey to Dublin was torture. I had two long hours to battle with my own mind. Use drugs, don't use drugs. Don't think about it, just do it, my thoughts were spinning around in my head. My heart was in my mouth when I scored the heroin. I knew the dealer and I was happy when she invited me into her flat to have a turn-on. I couldn't wait any longer to get the stuff into me. Once in the dealer's flat, I slipped back into the old me; that old familiar feeling of copping out of life and not caring any more was back in full swing. I don't remember much after that.

When I woke up, I was on a stretcher surrounded by children and worried onlookers. I was being wheeled into an ambulance. Then I saw Big Mick. How did *he* get here? I thought, but then everything went blank again.

When I eventually came around I realised that I had overdosed. The children had found me lying on the stairs in the block in Ballymun where I had gone to score. The dealer must have got a fright when I overdosed, dragged me out of her flat and left me there to die. When I hadn't come home from work, Mick knew exactly where I had gone. He drove to Dublin straight away. And when he saw the ambulance he knew that it was for me.

Once I recovered from my overdose, the weeks that followed saw me sneaking back and forward to Dublin and having sly turn-ons in Big Mick's house. But there was no fooling Big Mick. He could tell a mile off that I was back using drugs. He was heartbroken. But there was worse in store. Exposure to my addiction was simply too much for Mick. One day he came home from work and I knew. He walked through the front door with his eyes glossy and pinned to the back of his head. Ah no, was I seeing things? I thought. 'Please don't tell me that you've used,' I asked him, already knowing the answer. 'Oh my god, I don't believe this,' was all I could say.

I was disgusted with myself. Now Big Mick was back using after a full ten years being clean and it was all my fault. What did I expect when I was using right under his nose? I felt sick to my stomach when I looked at him. I loved Big Mick. I needed Big Mick. And he couldn't fall apart on me now.

Deep down I knew that getting involved romantically with Big Mick wasn't right. At times I had even admitted this to him. He had become something of a crutch for me. I was totally dependent on him for everything and I was responsible for dragging him down. We both fell apart. Big Mick drank every day and drugged himself into oblivion: the only time we left the house was to travel to Dublin to score some heroin.

Then one morning I found Big Mick lying on the floor in a heap. He was withering away. A shell of the man that he used to be. With a knife in his hand and surrounded by empty bottles of spirits, he was threatening to kill himself. After wrestling the knife from his hand, I had no choice but to call our neighbour for help. That morning was a very sad sight to see. Big Mick was admitted to a mental hospital.

———

The weeks that followed were the darkest of my life. Mick was gone and I was left alone in his house. Everything that I looked at reminded me of him and the damage that I had done. Big Mick had told me not to blame myself for his relapse. He said that he was big and hairy enough to make his own decisions and that it had been a long time coming anyway. But I didn't believe him.

I tried to soothe my own guilt by praying. But using drugs and praying just didn't mix. It was a recipe for disaster. My mind was consumed with negativity: as far as I was concerned God had left me alone, only to be replaced by demons. They were there, I was convinced of it. I couldn't see them, but I could hear them and I could feel their presence. They were following me everywhere I went and watching every movement I made. I was paralysed with fear. I spent most of my time in bed with the covers pulled over my head. 'You're not going mad, you're not going mad,' I told myself over and over again. But I was. Suicide was beginning to look very appealing. All that was left for me to do now was to join Big Mick in the nut-house. And that is what I did. I voluntarily signed myself into a mental institution.

So that was the end of myself and Big Mick. Like everything else in my life, it had ended badly. All I knew was that I had to leave the man alone. I knew that his family were there to support him and that the further he was away from me, the better it was for him. My family had no idea that I was in a mental institution. They really didn't need to know. I just needed to be left alone, locked up into a safe place, where I couldn't hurt myself or anyone else.

For the first few days I was heavily medicated, spending most of my time in bed and slipping in and out of consciousness. In my mind I was in the right place. Amongst my own people. I found great freedom in this. I was a nut-case and now nothing was expected of me.

Sometimes during the night the woman in the cubicle next to me would sneak into my cubicle. I had vaguely overheard the nurses calling the woman by the name of Theresa. She was an old woman from Mullingar and I had the feeling that she was harmless. She would sit by my bed and she would mumble prayers over my head. She must have known that I badly needed them. But I hardly even acknowledged the woman. I was too afraid to look at her and most times I would just pretend that I was asleep. She would stay there until the nurses came to take her away to give her her medication or her electric shock treatment. I always knew when Theresa got her electric shock treatment. She would seem brain-dead as she shuffled aimlessly around the ward, speaking incoherently to herself. I felt sorry for her and I wondered where her family were and what had happened to her that she had ended up in a place like this.

After a few days in hospital, I began to come back to my senses. The institution was exactly as I had imagined it to be. It had dreary green walls with bars on the windows and not one person seemed to have a light on in their heads. Maybe I looked the same to them. But deep down in my heart I knew that I wasn't cut out for a place like this. I wasn't mentally disturbed: I was just having a breakdown brought on by the stress of coping with my addiction. But I had no-one else to turn to and nowhere else to go. Experience had taught me that no matter where I went, nothing would change. Any place that I ran to, or any situation that I got myself into, always ended in a shambles, with others being hurt in the process. There was no way out for me. No matter what I tried, my addiction always got the better of me.

So I decided to stay put in the laughter academy. I practically lived in the smoking room, becoming familiar to most of the patients who came in to top up on their daily intake of nicotine. Most of them seemed surprisingly normal and even intelligent at times. I was beginning to think that half of them were only pretending to be mad. Maybe they were just like myself, looking for a break from the real world, having a rest and gathering some ground until they found the strength to face reality again.

This wasn't the case for Rosemary. She was a regular in the smoking room. She couldn't have been more than twenty. The first time I met her she came stumbling over to the bench beside me and introduced herself. 'Heya, what's your name?' she asked me as she took a seat.

'Rachael,' I told her.

'My name is Rosemary. Very pleased to meet you,' she said with a blank look in her eyes, medicated up to the hilt. Then Rosemary proceeded to tell me her whole life story. She told me that she was an only child from a family in the midlands. Her mother had died when she was only a child and her father was left to raise her on his own. He couldn't cope with the death of his wife and he took heavily to the drink. Rosemary told me that her father had taken his wife's death out on her: he had sexually abused her on a regular basis and he beat her up for no apparent reason. Then, when he couldn't take it any more, he signed Rosemary into a mental institution. 'He somehow managed to convince the doctors that *I* was the one who was mad,' she said. 'I ended up going mad in the end. This place would do that to anyone. I've been here since I was sixteen,' she continued. 'And since then, they just keep giving me medication. I'm doing much better now, though. They let me out a few times a week to do my course in art.'

I felt sad listening to Rosemary's story. I wasn't even sure if she was telling the truth, but she had opened my eyes to something. Whatever had happened to Rosemary had been so traumatic that she had no choice but to stay in a mental institution possibly for the rest of her life. But I did have a choice. I always had a choice. It didn't feel like I had a choice when I was actively using drugs, but once I got clean I had the freedom to choose whether I used or not. I remembered what somebody once told me in Narcotics Anonymous. 'A relapse happens long before the addict picks up the drug. It happens first in your mind, then in your behaviours. In order to get fucked, you have to get into the right position.' This saying made so much sense to me now.

I had certainly gotten myself into the right position. I had moved from Ballymun into a house in the middle of nowhere. The only support I had was from Big Mick who was in recovery himself and with no supports of his own. I had no means or tools to tackle my addiction. I had allowed my own negative thoughts to totally control my life. No wonder I had gone back using drugs. I didn't belong in a mental institution: I just needed treatment for my addiction.

After the first time I spoke to Rosemary, I began to write in my diary again. Writing always seemed to help me. Once I had all my thoughts out in the open and down on paper, I could see things much more clearly. In the end I came to the conclusion that I needed to go back into treatment.

Chapter 13 ∾

| MY LAST CHANCE

Here I was once again, standing at the gates of the Rutland Centre and, for the first time in my life, I was going into treatment *for myself*. I wasn't going in order to get my family off my back, or to have a little break from drugs. This time I was on my own and I genuinely wanted to learn how to live my life drug-free.

My heart was in my mouth as I dragged my suitcases up the long driveway. 'This is it now, Rachael,' I told myself with determination. 'It's time to lay all your shit out on the table and get really honest with yourself.' I knew what to expect from the Rutland Centre. It would be as tough as I made it: this was the last time I would do this and I wasn't going to hold back on anything. It was really make or break for me.

It was 2002 and it had been six years since I had last been in the Ruts. I was nothing but a child the last time I had been here and I really thought that I knew it all. This time round, all I knew was that I knew nothing. Nothing of any value, anyway.

The Rutland hadn't changed one bit. Everything still looked the same. Most of the old staff were still there, except for my counsellors, Jimmy and Marie. Even 'Supergran' was still there, one of the nurses, who had always been my favourite. Her face lit up when she saw me. 'Ah, would ye look who's back, it's Trouble,' she said as she gave me a big hug. Supergran introduced me to all of the clients. They were of all ages, from all backgrounds. Many of them were very well-to-do men and women who had problems with either alcohol or gambling. I spent the rest of my first day casually getting to know the other clients, but the next day I was thrown into the deep end and was placed into my first group session, in a large room that had once been a ballroom.

I could feel my heart thumping in my chest as I took my seat in the circle. I was relieved to find that I wasn't the only woman there. There was another young girl named Siobhán in the group. She looked so beautiful with her glossy blonde hair and clear skin. I wondered what she was in for. It couldn't have been the heroin. She just didn't have that look. The rest of the group were all men. I was so nervous now that I couldn't look any of them in the eye.

The two counsellors took their seats and they introduced themselves as Ann and Ultan. 'Ok, let's get started,' said Ultan with a grin on his face. 'We have a new addition to our group today. Rachael, you're very welcome! Now the group are going to take turns to introduce themselves to you.'

'I'll go first,' said one of the men. 'Hi, Rachael, my name is Timmy. You're very welcome to the group. All I can say is that this is a really good group. I've personally got so much out of it. You'll get back what you put in. I'm in here for the drink and I only have a few weeks left. But as I said, you're very welcome.' Timmy was a nervous kind of fella, built like an ox. He reminded me of a child in a man's body.

'Thanks, Timmy,' I told him.

'Hi, Rachael. My name is Siobhán. You're very welcome. I'm also here for my alcohol addiction and I have to say, this group is amazing. I've got a great sense of camaraderie here and I've made some really good friends as well. So don't be afraid to open up.' Siobhán was so cool. She spoke to me with such ease and confidence. 'Thanks, Siobhán.'

'How's it going, Rachael? I'm Dan and I'm an alcoholic and a drug addict. I'm only new here myself, but you're very welcome.' I liked Dan straight away. He seemed totally down to earth, somebody I could talk to. I knew that he was an alcoholic before he had even told me: he had a big red nose with broken veins on his face and he looked as though he was still suffering from the DTS. 'Thanks, Dan.'

'How'ya, Rachael, I'm Sam and I'm a compulsive gambler. You're very welcome.' Sam wasn't a bad-looking fella. He reminded me of my uncle Jonathon. He was around the same age as me, placid-looking and well-mannered.

'Emm, my name is Jim. You're very welcome. I'm actually cross-addicted. Drink, drugs, gambling. I'm here for them all.' Jim appeared to be in his early twenties and he was very well spoken, but he had a mischievous look in his eyes that told me he was only getting started in his addiction. There and then I made a mental note to watch out for Jim. Regardless of what Siobhán had said, I wasn't here to make friends: I was here to get myself well, and nobody was going to drag me down.

'Ok, Rachael, do you want to say a bit about yourself before we start the group?' Ultan offered.

Jaysus, I thought, I was knackered already after that introduction and I wasn't about to waffle on. 'Well, this is my second time in here. I'm a bit of a sucker for punishment as you can tell, but I plan on making this my last time here.'

'So what's so different this time round? What has changed?' asked Ann, the other counsellor. A glamorous woman, possibly in her mid-forties, I immediately knew by Ann's soft, soothing voice that she was the good cop.

'*I've* changed,' I told her. 'A lot has happened since the last time that I was here and I've definitely hit rock bottom.'

Ann accepted what I said with a nod and she left it at that. 'Ok, thanks, Rachael.' 'Thanks, Rachael,' the group echoed her. Ultan then moved the group onto Dan and he began to question him about all the moving he'd done from country to country in an attempt to escape his addiction. That's me all over, I thought to myself as I listened to Dan go on about his escapes. Even though I'd been helped by my family, I had eagerly kept moving to avoid coming to terms with my real problems. I knew there and then that I was definitely in the right place.

The group continued for another two hours—enough to drain the life out of anyone. I was grateful that I had been given a methadone crash course in the mental institution. Even though I was still a little bit 'ropey', my withdrawal symptoms weren't half as bad as they had been in Community Cenacolo. I just felt like I had a little bit of a flu. That's what I told myself anyway. Another week or so and I would be brand new.

After the group it was time for dinner. Jack, the elusive chef, was still working in the kitchen. Jack was renowned for his hearty home-made meals, but I had yet to meet the man. He would do his job and quickly disappear. I knew that for a lot of the clients, when all else failed, their main incentive to stay in the Rutland was Jack's divine cooking creations. I had always been amazed at how thirty-odd people could fit into such a small dining area. Once the scramble for the food was over and somebody had said grace, the only sound that could be heard was people munching on their food.

If anything worked up an appetite, it was group therapy. 'Stuffing the feelings' we called it. We would all stuff our feelings, except for the people who had eating disorders. Jack would cook them their own special meal, depending on their specific needs. My heart would go out to them as they sat with one of the nurses who would closely monitor every spoonful they ate. I was baffled at how those people could cope with such a disorder: it would be like me trying to monitor and 'control' my drug use. I knew that, no matter how much awareness or information I had about my addiction, that would be impossible. When dinner was over we were allowed to take a break until two o'clock. Then we were back into our groups for another session.

The regime in Rutland was in many ways strict and relentless. I was told in advance exactly what type of clothing I was allowed to wear. Nothing too revealing or low-cut. There were too many hormones and emotions flying around the place for that. We were allowed to bring a certain amount of toiletries and make-up, but we could only wear a little: there was to be no hiding behind masks. Under no circumstances were we allowed to listen to our own music or watch the television, not unless we were given permission to do so. Sam explained to me that the television rule especially applied to the gamblers and the alcoholics. With the amount of Budweiser ads and horse-racing programmes that were on, it was just too much temptation for them. I knew exactly what he meant. If I was watching an ad on the television that had a needle with heroin dripping from it and some man saying, 'China White, king of turn-ons', I would have no hope of staying clean.

———

And so, back into the group for another session. This time the focus was on Sam. 'How's the head today, Sam?' Ultan asked him.

'Ah, I'm still the same. I just can't stop gambling.'

I didn't know what he was talking about. How could he still be gambling in here? I wondered.

'I'm gambling on stupid things,' Sam continued, 'and the more I try to stop, the more I keep on doing it.'

'What are you gambling on?'

'Stupid things, like who's going to sit in what chair first. It's mad. If I was left on my own with a fucking fly, I'd somehow find a way to gamble on it.'

'What's the pay-off if you win the bet in your head?' asked Ultan.

'I feel good.'

'And what if you lose?'

'I feel bad. But it's just anything that will take me away from how I'm really feeling.' Now I knew what Sam meant. Once he was living in his head, he never had to really *feel* anything.

'What do you do with these thoughts?' Ultan probed.

'I don't know. Nothing really,' Sam replied.

'Well I'd suggest that when you get these thoughts in your head, you go and tell somebody,' said Ultan. 'If you don't, they will only manifest themselves as actions. At least if you tell someone, you might see them more for what they are. And I would say that for anyone here who is having obsessive thoughts: you go and tell somebody.' Everyone nodded compliantly. There was that old language again. 'Manifestation of thoughts', 'obsessions', 'feelings'. It was like a secret language used only by people who were in recovery. It wasn't a language that you would use with normal civilians. They would think you were mad and they would probably run a mile.

'Ok, Sam, thanks for being so honest,' said Ultan. A silence fell over the group room and I kept my eyes firmly on the ground, hoping they wouldn't ask me anything. As if reading my mind, Ann addressed me: 'Rachael, how are you getting on so far?'

'Emm, I'm settling in really well, but I'm still a bit afraid about opening up to the group.'

'Have you ever done a First Step?' Ann asked.

'Yeah, I did one the last time that I was here, but to be honest I made a bit of a gangster movie out of the whole thing.' I had made my life sound like something from *The Godfather*, rather than focusing on the truth of my addiction.

'Ok, you can start the First Step today. You know you can never write too much on this, so don't hold back.' The First Step came to light from the Big Book of Alcoholics Anonymous, where the steps towards recovery were written down. The First Step read: 'We admitted that we were powerless over our alcoholism and our lives had become unmanageable.' To complete the First Step in the Rutland we had to write answers to a series of questions that were designed for us to recognise how our addiction worked. The questions were searching and difficult and I knew that when I read out my First Step, my darkest secrets would be revealed to the group. I was dreading it, but I knew that it had to be done.

That evening I got started. I sat in the ballroom with one of the new guys, Chris. It was his first time in treatment and we clicked with each other straight away. He was to become one of my most trusted friends. I was already struggling to write, so I decided to take a break. I was sitting in the conservatory and I noticed that Timmy was hovering by the door.

'Are you alright, Timmy? You don't look the best.'

'Not really,' he admitted, his head held low. 'I've to read out my First Step tomorrow and I'm really afraid that everyone's going to judge me. I'm afraid that *you're* going to judge me.'

'Timmy, believe me, I'm no-one to judge *you*. Wait till you hear my First Step, you'll know what I mean then. Don't worry about it. Sure you'll probably never see half of these people again. You're doing this for yourself, aren't you?' The purpose of the First Step was not to embarrass you in front of group, but to face some tough truths about your addiction.

'Yes I am. But I've done some really bad stuff.' I knew that Timmy had problems. He had been heavily confronted earlier in group because he had blatantly refused to make breakfast for the staff and the clients. He had stomped his feet and stormed out of the kitchen, without giving an explanation as to why he wouldn't do his chore. Eventually the truth came out that Timmy had serious issues with authority figures. He didn't like being told what to do. Seemingly he was still haunted by memories of being in the army.

No amount of assurance that I gave Timmy could ease his worries. I couldn't be *that* bad, I thought. Anyway, I had enough on my own plate. I was missing Big Mick badly. I had heard that he had got out of hospital and was recovering really well. He had tried to make contact with me in the Rutland, but I just wasn't ready to speak to him yet.

After telling the group about our relationship, the counsellors suggested that Big Mick come up for Concerned Persons day. Big Mick knew me inside-out and the thought of him confronting me scared me half to death. But I agreed to do it anyway. It was arranged for Big Mick to be my first CP.

When the day arrived, I was really nervous about seeing Big Mick. He was a former client of the Rutland and he knew exactly how the groups worked. There wouldn't be any chance of him holding back on information.

I caught a glimpse of his tall frame and his green Gortex jacket. As usual, Big Mick had a cup of coffee in one hand and a Dunhill Light in the other. As soon as the prep group was over, I walked over to where he stood. He held his arms out to embrace me. That old familiar smell of Eternity for Men was there and I just wanted to stay there for ever. But I knew in my heart that there was no going back for myself and Big Mick.

'You're very welcome, Michael,' Ann opened the session. 'Would you like to tell us a little bit about Rachael and her addiction?'

'Well,' Mick began, 'I have always tried to be there for Rachael throughout her addiction. But I've always felt that Rachael's real problems lay with the relationship, or lack of relationship, with her mother and her father. Her grandmother has always been there, but I don't think that was ever enough for Rachael. It's as though she has always tried to replace those relationships with the drugs.'

Mick knew all the right things to say, I thought, but then he dropped the bombshell. 'And if I'm to be entirely honest, she did it with the prostitution as well.' I had told Mick all about my life on Baggot Street, all the horrible details. But I couldn't believe he was now telling everyone else. I could feel myself going red. I hadn't had the chance to tell the group about the prostitution yet. I was planning on doing that in my First Step. Mick continued, 'I have always seen potential in Rachael and it was frustrating knowing what she was doing and not being able to help her. But

I didn't take it personally because I understand myself what it's like.'

'Yourself and Rachael were in a relationship together, right?' said Ann.

'Yeah, we've been together over the last two years. She was doing so well in the beginning, but then she went off the rails again. It broke my heart. You know how much I love you, don't you?' he said, looking right into my eyes. 'I would've married you, but you kept on saying that you were too dependent on me. I was so angry with you when you used and it killed me to see you so upset all the time. But I tried my best. I really did. I never meant for things to turn out the way they did. I'm really sorry.'

What was *he* sorry for? He'd done nothing wrong. I felt like crying. I genuinely loved Big Mick, but in all the wrong ways. He was more like a father figure to me.

'Do you think Rachael used you?' asked Ultan.

Big Mick had to think about that one. 'I don't know if "used" is the right word. She leaned on me and *I* let her. But yeah, I think that she was with me for the wrong reasons.'

'And how does that feel?'

'I don't think she meant to hurt me. She didn't go out of her way to use me,' Mick explained.

'Be honest, Michael,' urged Ultan.

'Ok, I was really hurt knowing that Rachael was with me for all the wrong reasons. But I hoped that she would eventually grow to love me. It hurt that I was never enough.'

Jesus, I was such a little bitch. I had thought about nothing but myself. I had expected Big Mick's life to revolve around mine and I never really thought about how I might be affecting him. I was shocked when he relapsed, but it wasn't until then that I realised what I was doing to him. That was all Big Mick had to say. But I knew that the group would get stuck into me later on. That was how it worked.

That day I felt sad saying goodbye to Big Mick. He told me that he and the little house in the country were missing me and that I was always welcome back. 'Co-dependency and all,' he said, always being the joker.

————

The intense group therapy and the constant activity was really knocking me for six. I wasn't used to a routine and I seemed to be permanently tired. But for the first time in ages I was getting a decent night's sleep. Those negative spiritual attachments seemed to have disappeared and my head was beginning to slow down. I had peace at last. I realised that the mistake I had made the last time with the prayer and meditation was that I had brought it to the extreme: I had turned the prayers into an obsessive chant which really disturbed my mind. I had become as hooked on prayer as I had been on heroin. But it was important for me to pray and meditate. I just had to find a balance. And I also had to find a quiet place to do it. I was too paranoid to pray in my bedroom in case somebody would walk in and catch me. Then they would definitely think that I was mad. So I decided to go into the bathroom.

Just as I was drifting off to the sound of my own mantra, the bathroom door swung open. 'Oh, Jaysus, I'm sorry,' said this young girl whose face was really familiar. I knew her well, but I couldn't for the life of me remember how.

'Rachael?' she said, as I quickly jumped to my feet.

'Where do I know you from?' I asked her, red in the face.

'D'ye not remember me? Jessica! We lived in a squat together out in Ballymun.' Now I remembered. But Jessica looked so different. She had obviously taken a beating from the heroin, but she was still very pretty. She was a tiny little thing, with a long plum-coloured bob. She was chatty, straightforward and full of nervous energy. We were going to share a room together, she said. I wasn't sure if this would be a good thing or a bad thing. Only time would tell.

———

Today I could relax because all I had to do was listen to Timmy read out his First Step, the one that had caused him so much difficulty. The famous box of tissues was placed on the floor in the middle of the circle. Timmy sat in his chair, stiffly holding his A4 pages, as the group took turns to smile at him in encouragement.

'Ok, Timmy, you can start reading out your step,' said Ann. Timmy began to give the group different examples of how he had experienced being powerless over his addiction. He spoke of the time when he drank alcohol against his own will, and the hurt that he caused his family. He told us how his alcoholism had progressed from an early age and how it had got worse when he had left the army. To me it was all very normal stuff for someone who was an alcoholic and I wondered why Timmy had been so afraid to read it out. Within a very short space of time, Timmy was finished reading out his First Step, but I just knew that he wasn't being completely honest. You can't bullshit a bullshitter.

'Timmy, you've skipped some questions,' said Ultan.

Beads of sweat were trickling down Timmy's forehead. 'Oh, I know. I got stuck on that question about how my addiction manifests itself. I didn't really understand it.'

'It means in what areas does your addiction go? When is it most visible and how?' There was a long pause. 'Why do you think you started drinking in the first place, Timmy?' Ultan asked. 'What were you running from?'

Everyone looked at Timmy. He was wiping invisible fluff off his trousers. 'I don't know. Myself maybe.'

'What's so bad about Timmy that he has to run from himself?' Ultan continued.

Timmy leaned his head on his hand. 'I just can't stand myself, Ultan.'

'Why, Timmy?' Another long pause. 'Because I was abused, that's why. And now I've become the abuser.' Everyone's eyes were shifting from one person to the other. And I was beginning to feel really uncomfortable.

'How d'you mean you've become the abuser?' Ultan was homing in on Timmy now. He was sitting on the edge of his chair with his head held low, as though he was trying to get down to Timmy's level.

'I have become an abuser. Things got so bad that I began to flash at women.' All the eyes were shifting around the room again.

Ultan didn't seem fazed. 'Do you want to talk about this, Timmy?'

Timmy cupped his face in his hands. 'No, I can't, I can't,' he said. 'I feel so ashamed.'

'Can you describe the shame, Timmy?'

Ah, Ultan, will you just stop, I screamed at him in my head. Now Timmy was tearing at his face and he was no longer with us in the group room. He seemed to be gone somewhere else in his mind. 'I know what it's like to be abused and it's not fucking nice. How could I do that to those women?'

'How did it make you feel at the time, Timmy?'

'I felt powerful and ashamed at the same time, but then I just felt empty. I can feel it everywhere.' Timmy was tearing at his arms now and his face was distorted.

I couldn't listen to this any more. I was on the verge of bolting out the door. I felt nauseous and I wanted to vomit. Memories of my own sexual deviances came rushing to the front of my mind: the dark lanes of Baggot Street, the dirty perverted men, desperately trying to fill themselves up at any cost. The seediness of it all. The devastation of giving that part of myself away, just for a bag of heroin. And the emptiness. Yes, I knew that feeling only too well. That big sore hole right in the middle of my chest that nothing could fill and the loneliness that no man or woman could take away. 'Fuck you anyway, Timmy,' I wanted to lash out at him. To me, he represented all those men to whom I had given my power. The group room was beginning to spin and I was finding it harder to breathe. Timmy was sobbing uncontrollably. Ultan stopped provoking him and he allowed him to cry.

——

The lights in the NA—Narcotics Anonymous—room were cruel and unforgiving. I was in no humour for an NA meeting, especially after the group that we had, but it was compulsory for the clients to go to their meetings so I had no choice. Myself, Chris and Jessica huddled together down the back of the room and I just wished I were invisible. I was struck by the numbers of addicts, now in recovery, who had come to the meeting to carry their message, about forty of them, looking so well, as though they hadn't a care in the world. 'I AM RESPONSIBLE…,' it said in big black writing on the wall.

The meeting started and for about thirty minutes a man spoke about his experiences with drugs and his recovery. He had also done a stint in the Rutland and he was a long time clean. He couldn't emphasise enough how important it was for him to have the support of NA throughout his recovery. 'I didn't come in here brimming with hope and all those good things. I was hopeless, homeless, helpless, unemployable and desperate. I hadn't a clue what people were on about when they used the words like "surrendering to a power greater than myself," or "powerlessness". But I stuck with it, putting one foot in front of the other. And now my life has done a complete turn-around.' This man was a graphic designer with his own home and he liked to travel the world taking pictures. If he can do it, then so can I, I thought to myself. From here onwards I would be on the look-out for a good woman who could be my sponsor, to guide me through the programme and to support me in my recovery.

After listening to different people speak, my spirits lifted. These meetings really do work, I thought. I knew after that first meeting that I would have to commit myself to NA if I wanted to get what those people had. I would give it a bash and try to do the suggested things. I had nothing to lose.

Chapter 14 ∾

| FACING THE TRUTH

Even though the regime in the Rutland was demanding, it wasn't all group therapy in the Centre. At weekends we would gather together in the television room for a game of charades. Other times we would have a sing-along in the kitchen as we belted on the pots and pans. There were yoga and dance classes, and when we were really bored we would have an egg-and-spoon race in the garden, which usually resulted in the neighbours complaining about the noise. I would have done anything for a laugh and to get away from the heightened emotion of the group.

I had heard from somebody that my old counsellor Jimmy Judge was coming in to do a workshop with us. Shit, if anyone scared me, it was Jimmy Judge. He was the most gifted counsellor that I had ever come across. And when I was in his presence I felt completely transparent.

The first time I met Jimmy I was only twelve years old. It was one year before I started on the heroin. My school class had been taken to the Youth Action Project in Ballymun for a drugs awareness day. I remember being struck by Jimmy's tattoos. He had funny cartoon characters on both of his hands. One of them was of Daffy Duck. He was only a handful of a man, standing at around five foot five. He showed my class a video about the effects of drugs and the damage that they did, but I took very little notice. None of it applied to me as far as I was concerned, even though I was smoking hash, drinking alcohol, taking acid and dabbling with ecstasy. Being a junkie just wasn't something that I aspired to be. So I didn't have to listen. Maybe I should have listened.

'I can only imagine what he has up his sleeve,' I whispered to Jessica now. All the clients had filled the television room and we were sitting in a large circle.

'Right, so, we'll get started, will we?' Jimmy said enthusiastically, doing a little jump. 'Ok, everyone on your feet. Now, I want you to give every part of your body a good shake. Do a little dance if you want. C'mon, don't be afraid to shake it all out.' We all did as Jimmy said and I felt like a right eegit.

'Now, open your mouth as wide as you can and scream, but without making any noise...'

'What did I tell you,' I whispered to Jessica.

'Now you can sit down. I want you to pick two animals. One that represents your addiction and one that represents your recovery. Have you got that?'

Everyone nodded and Jimmy continued, 'Now, I want you to stand up here, one by one and act out your animal.'

No fucking way was I going to do that, I thought. I had an image to uphold here.

Everyone was moaning and groaning. 'Ah c'mon, it's only a bit of fun. Who'll go first? What's your name?' he said pointing to Michael, one of the clients.

'Emm, Michael, but I'm not doing it. I'm only new here myself.'

'Ahm, you might do it later on. What's your name?' he pointed to Timmy.

'I'm Timmy.'

'Good man, Timmy, you'll go first, won't you?' I was surprised that Timmy agreed. But he had said that he would make more of an effort.

They were like Little and Large standing there together: Timmy towering over Jimmy. 'Right, Timmy, what animal did you pick for your addiction?' Jimmy said cheerfully.

Timmy didn't know what to be doing with himself. 'I picked a gorilla.'

'Alright, so do a gorilla.'

Timmy was puce in the face now and he couldn't stop laughing. Jimmy laughed along with him. 'It's ok, go on.' Then Timmy put his fist to his chest and he start pounding it and making noises as though he were King Kong. Everyone thought that this was hilarious at first but then Timmy suddenly stopped laughing and a strange look came over his face. He began to thump himself harder and harder and his voice had changed. He was screaming now. I had never in my life heard such a noise. Nobody was laughing any more. I noticed that Jessica was nearly sitting on top of me, with a firm grip on my arm.

But Jimmy was only getting started. 'Hi, Rachael,' he addressed me. 'Do you want to do it?'

'No, you're alright, Jimmy. I'm not doing it.'

'Ah c'mon, you know it'll do you the world of good!' He reached out his hand for me to take. 'Don't be afraid. I'll even do it with you.'

He was putting me on the spot and I couldn't say no. 'What animal did you pick for your addiction?'

I noticed that Jimmy had a lovely light in his eyes. 'A lion.'

'Why did you pick a lion?'

'Because it's fierce and powerful. That's how my addiction feels.'

'Very good. So what does a lion do?'

I was so conscious of everyone staring at me. 'Ah, I'm not doing it, Jimmy.'

'C'mon, we'll do it together.' Jimmy got down on his hands and knees. So I copied him. 'Rarr,' Jimmy growled, urging me to do the same.

'Rarr,' I growled back. Then Jimmy began to chase me around the room on all fours. I was trying my best to laugh it off, but I just couldn't seem to hold myself together. I was so embarrassed that I began to cry. I had no idea why, but my mother had suddenly come into my head. Jimmy took me by the hands and he picked me up off the ground. Then he put his face right up to mine and he blocked the room out with his hands. He was way too close for comfort and now I was seriously freaked out.

'Forget about everyone in the room. Why did you start to cry?'

'I was mortified and then I just thought of my ma.'

'How do you feel about your ma?'

'I feel that she doesn't love me and I don't know why. I'm angry with her.'

'I want you now to go around each and every person in this room and speak to them as if they're your ma. Tell her how angry you are.'

'I can't, Jimmy.'

'Try, Rachael.'

I did try. I really did. But something inside me kept telling me that I was betraying my own mother. I just couldn't let go. I couldn't do this to my mother with all these people whom I hardly even knew. I tried. I went around the room, around every person in the group and spoke to them, but the words weren't real; I was only doing it to please Jimmy. Nonetheless, my session with Jimmy was the most powerful experience that I had in the Rutland and one that I would never forget.

———

At the same time as working things out in group, I was beginning to feel more and more at home in the NA meetings. Everyone seemed very friendly and I had even mustered up the courage to speak once or twice. Tonight was the first time that a woman was in the chair, Katriona. I was mesmerised by her. She seemed so relaxed as she sat in front of everyone, smiling and waving to most of the other members. She couldn't have being much older than myself. She had long blonde hair and a warm open face. Then she began to speak. She told us all about her traumatic childhood, her drug use and her recovery. Her story was scarily similar to mine. Her presence and the way she held herself captivated me. And I *really* wanted to have the confidence that she had. I just had to ask her to be my sponsor. But I didn't know how. What if she says no? I thought. I'd die.

When the meeting was over I anxiously floated around her, but she seemed to be busy talking to everyone else. 'Just do it,' I told myself. And after going over the whole thing in my mind several times, I eventually got the courage to approach her. I told her how much I had enjoyed listening to her. Then I just blurted it out. 'Would you be able to be my sponsor?'

'Yeah, no problem,' she replied. I could hardly believe my luck. Perhaps one day, I thought, I might be Katriona—confident, assured, in touch with herself. For the moment I was very pleased with myself simply to have taken the first step and plucked up the courage to ask her to sponsor me. Katriona has been my rock ever since and has supported me through the worst of times and the best.

I was aware that I was blessed to be in a group of people who were as serious as I was about staying clean. And it was in listening to the others speak so honestly about their addiction that more was being revealed to me about myself. I had been blown away by Timmy's First Step and his courage in telling the truth. Now, I had to take a leaf out of his book and do the same. It was time for me to share my First Step with the group.

On the day of reckoning I was terrified. I could feel my stomach doing somersaults as I joined the circle in the group room. Then Ann gave me the nod to begin. I told the group about how my addiction affected me mentally. How it distorted my thinking and made me believe things about myself that weren't true, that I was a failure and that, deep down at the core of my being, I was a bad person. I thought everyone around me instinctively knew this, which made me feel even worse about myself. I was different to everyone else in the worst way possible, but I couldn't put my finger on how. I spoke about my obsession with drugs: every waking second was spent thinking about how I would get drugs, where I would use them and how I would feel when I got them into me. Even my dreams were ambushed by visions of drug-use. During the times that I was drug-free, the obsession was still there, but it wasn't an obsession with drugs, but about myself. Morning, noon and night I was living in my head. Thinking about myself and of how I looked and how I sounded. How others perceived me and whether they liked me or not. If I thought they didn't like me, I would become somebody that they did like. I had a thousand faces for a thousand different people. I could be anyone that you wanted me to be.

I continued to say that, if I wasn't obsessed with myself, I was obsessed with prayer and meditation. 'Please God, do this for me. Please God, don't let this or that happen. If I do this, God will reward me. If I do that, God will punish me. It was mental torture,' I told the group, explaining how I had replaced an addiction to drugs with an addiction to God.

'I am an emotional cripple,' I told them. 'My emotions are so warped that I can't tell my arse from my elbow.' I told them that I loved how the drugs made me feel numb, but only for a while. Even when I used drugs now, I was bombarded with all these emotions that I just couldn't cope with. I was riddled with fear, guilt and shame. I had no idea of how to express any sort of anger and it was even harder for me to smile. My spirit seemed to be dead. It had been crushed so many times by myself and others that I could never see myself being truly happy again. I had forgotten what it was like to be happy anyway.

I then took a deep breath. It was time to tell the group just how powerless I was over my addiction. About all the things I had done in the grip of heroin. Like the time I robbed my grandmother's wedding ring. I had only started taking drugs and

I promised myself that I would never rob my family. Especially my grandmother, the only one who loved me unconditionally, I thought. I repaid this by stealing her precious ring. I badly needed to get money for drugs and the thought came into my head that I would get at least twenty pounds for it. I remember a voice in my head saying, 'No, don't do it, don't do it. You know that's not right.' But I felt that I genuinely couldn't stop myself, that I had no power or control. In the end I took my grandmother's ring and I will never forget how she cried when she realised that it was gone. I hid the ring in one of my teddy bears until I could smuggle it out of the house, and when I heard her crying I pretended to help her to find it.

It was at this point that I looked around the group room at the clients. None of them had walked out on me yet. They weren't scoffing at me or laughing at me. So I carried on, telling them about the times when I broke into other people's homes, or shop-lifted, or sold my family's clothes to buy drugs. I knew in my heart that this wasn't right, stealing from people who were asleep in their beds. I was doing it against my own will. Once I was using drugs I just couldn't stop myself. Every time that I did something I said I would never do, it became easier for me to push the goal-posts back further and further, until I was left with virtually no morals or principles.

Then I got to the prostitution part, the deep, dark shame at the centre of it all. The one thing that no amount of excuses could seem to justify. I was shaking in my chair at this point. But I had to keep going. 'Selling my body was the last thing I wanted to do,' I told them. 'I got to the point where I didn't care any more; that voice in my head, the good part of me, begged me to stop. But I just couldn't.' Now, I felt wide open to the group. Completely exposed. I hated talking about my sexuality. It made me feel so ashamed. In my mind, selling my body was worse than anything else I had ever done.

I didn't go into too much detail about how I prostituted myself.

Just telling the group that I had *done* it was a huge risk for me to take. 'But I know for a fact that I wouldn't have done it if I wasn't on drugs. I only did it because I had a habit to feed,' I concluded to the group. That was that out of the way and I was relieved that I had told the truth. I was getting it all out into the open. I went into detail about the damage I had done to my family and anyone I came in contact with. I finished reading out my First Step by admitting to the group that I was unmanageable in every single area of my life and that I simply couldn't live like this any more. I was ready to take the next necessary step to help me to stay clean. I felt an overwhelming sense of relief. I had finally admitted that I couldn't do it on my own. I couldn't overcome my addiction by sheer willpower, or by prayer. I needed their help and I was asking for it now. I was admitting for the first time that I was truly powerless over my addiction. Now, I could begin my recovery.

My First Step completed and having followed the rigorous regime in the Rutland, the day had finally come for me to leave. After giving my little speech and saying my thank yous, I was ready to go. This was it for me now. I was going out into the big bad world completely drug-free. I had a sponsor and had got a list of numbers from NA members and I was determined to stick to my plan of going to ninety meetings in ninety days.

My mother had come back from America and she and Philip had moved into a new apartment together. They invited me to come and live with them, but I was determined to stand on my own two feet. Anyway, I was far from ready to live with my mother. I would have to sort myself out first before I even attempted to have a relationship with her. So I got myself my own little flat on the southside of Dublin. It was the first place that I could call my own and it was perfect.

I hadn't once thought of using drugs, but it felt really strange being clean. My suit of armour was gone now and I no longer had the drugs to hide behind. It was as though I were walking around Dublin completely naked. All the group therapy that I had done left me feeling raw and I suddenly had a heightened awareness of myself. Everything seemed to overwhelm me. The bright lights of the city. The traffic. Other human beings. Jesus, I wondered, had I been dead? It was as if I had opened my eyes for the first time. I was noticing buildings for the first time. Even the sky looked different. I had been too stoned for too long and too ashamed to hold my head up high and look at the sky. I knew that I would have to be very careful. The slightest little thing could trigger a craving.

To help me, I was told to avoid people, places and things that I associated with my drug use. Katriona suggested that I wear a Walkman and a watch when I was walking around on my own, so if I bumped into one of my old mates who was on drugs, I could pretend not to hear them, or look at my watch and say that I had to be somewhere at a certain time. Upstairs on the bus was a no-go area: this was where all the active drug users sat and addiction was rampant. Many a time had I smoked gear, had turn-ons and sold robbed stuff upstairs at the back of the bus. Sitting up there now would be asking for trouble. These were some of the things that I would have to do if I wanted to stay clean.

My life at this time revolved solely around NA. I was learning how to live my life again and I was loving every minute of it. I couldn't believe it when I saw Tommy K still knocking around in NA. He had been in my group the first time I had been in the Rutland all those years ago and had got clean. I wondered what he had done to stay clean that I hadn't managed to do. The difference in him now was unbelievable. Tommy K could barely pull two words together in the Ruts. Now, he was doing service and chairs in NA and he seemed to know what he was talking about. It was as though Tommy K had never even touched a drug. He looked so healthy now and grown up. When he saw me he gave me a big hug. This was a first: he had never been the hugging type. Seeing him doing so well made me even more determined to stay clean.

For the first two months in NA, I was like a duck out of water. I had to constantly stay around members to avoid temptation. 'An addict on their own is bad company,' I was told. Stick with the winners. But I was very intimidated by the long-timers. The people who had been clean for years. I just couldn't relate to them. I felt so inadequate when I listened to them talking about their mortgages and their bills. These things just didn't apply to me. It was easier for me to hang around with Jessica and Chris, my friends from the Rutland. I could relax with them and just be myself.

We spent most of our time hanging around coffee shops with other newcomers, on a high just because we were alive and drug-free. But I was still very vulnerable. I could wear a Walkman and a watch and sit on the lower deck of the bus. I could attend daily NA meetings and hang around with clean, healthy people, but my biggest weakness was one I found harder to avoid.

Justin was just another recovering addict of whom I didn't take much notice at first. Katriona had warned me to stick with the women—she knew that I was vulnerable to men and she didn't want to see me being taken advantage of. But at this time I found it easier to talk to men, and, as Justin hung around with us, I began to notice what a nice guy he was. He seemed very quiet with a good head on his shoulders. He was easy to talk to and I could have a laugh with him as well. Over the weeks that passed I found myself thinking about Justin a lot. He was becoming more and more attractive to me every time I saw him. He paid me lots of attention and made me feel good about myself. And I liked how respectful he was towards me.

Katriona was worried when I told her about my attraction to Justin. 'Don't make the mistake again of getting into relationships for all the wrong reasons,' she cautioned. 'Your self-esteem is on the floor, you're lonely, you're hurting and you're clean only a wet day. Give yourself a break.' Katriona was right. I wasn't even sure why I wanted to be with Justin. And I knew in my heart that I wasn't ready. But against all the warnings I hooked up with him anyway.

My relationship with Justin started out really well. We spent a lot of our time together and I really enjoyed his company. But I knew that I had to keep my focus on my recovery. That was my priority. I tried to keep myself occupied by doing an after-care recovery group during the day. It would give me a reason to get out of bed and I would also have all the support and structure that I needed.

Five months had passed and I was still clean. I was still learning about NA and I was surprised at how well I seemed to be juggling my relationship with Justin and my recovery. So we began to spend more and more time with each other. But over time I started to notice that my priorities were changing: Justin was slowly but surely coming before my own recovery. Instead of meeting Katriona or going to NA, I was cuddling up with him. During the times that I did meet Katriona, I spoke to her at length about my relationship with Justin. Suspicious of my motives, she questioned me continuously about my reasons for being with him and what my 'pay-off' was. 'Why are you with Justin?' she would say. 'What attracts you to him?' I couldn't tell her; I had no idea. 'Is it the fact that he's still a little bit dysfunctional?' she probed. She was right. Justin was a bit dysfunctional, but then so was I. Most of us newcomers were. It was to be expected after years of drug use. 'You're still living in the madness, Rachael,' Katriona insisted. 'You're clean and crazy. You're hanging around coffee shops looking for any sort of escape from yourself. Your life is still completely unmanageable. You're missing days in your after-care recovery group. Your money is gone the minute you get it and you're in a relationship with someone who has stopped going to meetings and who just seems to be angry all the time. I think you need to stop and take a long hard look at *yourself*, not at Justin.'

Katriona always told me the truth, whether it was nice or not. I knew that she was right, but at the time I couldn't see how my attraction to men like Justin played a part in my addiction. I had a very low opinion of myself and I looked up to Justin because he had been clean longer than me. If anyone at all paid me attention like he did, I lapped it up. When I thought about what Katriona had said to me, I knew in my heart that I was making the same mistakes all over again and replacing drugs with other things, but I kept kidding myself that I would somehow make it work.

My relationship with Justin was not healthy, I knew that, and it was beginning to go pear-shaped. Justin was having problems with his family and he was like a walking volcano about to erupt. He was becoming increasingly paranoid about my whereabouts and my relationships with my male friends. One day when Justin asked me if I thought one of my male friends was attractive, I told the truth and I admitted that I did. I had been too honest for my own good. Justin couldn't handle this.

That night myself and Justin had a huge row. He was convinced that I was betraying him when I wasn't and every time I tried to leave his flat he would stand in my way. I couldn't believe that this was happening between us. I knew Justin was angry, but I never thought that he would treat me like this, shouting at me. He was scaring me. The argument was really getting nasty. We must have rowed for almost an hour. Things were said that should not have been said. Justin said things that hurt me deeply. And it went on and on. And the longer it went on, the more my confidence crumbled.

———

I thought that I was getting stronger, but after this row I realised that I was as fragile as ever. By the time Justin left I was a wreck.

My confidence in myself was gone. My self-esteem was on the floor.

————

All of my old demons resurfaced and with them an overwhelming urge to make myself feel good again. For some strange reason my mind kept reverting to the prostitution. I couldn't stop thinking about it. But I could no longer remember how bad it was. All I could think about was that powerful feeling I got when men paid me to have sex with them. I could always depend on my sexuality to make me feel good about myself. I suddenly found myself on a bus heading up to Baggot Street. I was so blinded by my own hurt that I couldn't remember when I had made the decision to go back up there. And I wasn't exactly sure *why* I was going. I hadn't really thought about it. All I knew was that I had this overriding urge to walk those dark streets just to see what was happening.

As I walked along the docks of the canal I noticed a bunch of flowers tied to one of the railings. They had a note hanging from them and, curious to see what it said, I walked over to the railings. Then I saw her name. The note read SINEAD. I knew Sinead well. She was a lovely girl, who worked the streets and had been murdered because of it, because she owed money to somebody. I felt a pang in my stomach and for a split second I realised what I was doing. Just go home; you don't have to do this, I told myself. But I had already crossed the line in my head and nothing could stop me now. That night I got in and out of many cars. But I didn't feel powerful. I just felt ashamed. So ashamed that I wanted to rip my insides out. But a part of me was satisfied because in my mind that was exactly what I deserved.

I was hanging by a thread and the only thing stopping me from using were my friends. I had noticed that the people whom I had *thought* were my friends suddenly weren't there any more, but others, whom I thought weren't my friends, were rallying around me. Jimmy Judge was there. He asked me if I wanted to see him as a friend or a counsellor. He could be either/or. But I had to choose which one. I knew I would be blessed to have Jimmy as a friend, but if he could be my counsellor I would benefit so much more. He also told me something that shocked me to the core—that as long as I continued to sell my body I was raping myself.

Another friend, Declan, was there. I had met him in the meetings and I had taken a shine to him from day one. We had gotten clean around the same time and I knew in my gut that he was one of the good ones. But in spite of Jimmy and Katriona and Declan, it was all too much for me to handle. I still hadn't used drugs yet, but I was holding on for dear life.

———

In the end, my friends weren't enough. It was only a matter of time before I went back using drugs. By now, filled with guilt and self-loathing, I had pushed *everyone* away from me—Jimmy, Declan, even Katriona, who had done everything in her power to help me. She was heartbroken when I started using drugs again, but eventually even she had to walk away. I had moved into a shabby little flat in the city centre and I began to work from there. I was still devastated over what had happened with Justin, but I tried to block it all out with as much drugs as possible. I acquired a taste for speedballs, heroin and cocaine mixed together. These two drugs contradict each other in their effects and they have the potential to kill you there and then. But I told myself that I didn't care. I would have done *anything* but feel.

It was at this time that I met Seán, whom I had known since my teenage years. He was a local boy and somebody I had time for. Now, we had the same drug dealer and we always seemed to be scoring at the same time, but unlike my previous boyfriends, Seán was a gentle soul, very easy to be around. He was a loner and so was I. We connected in our loneliness.

I began to use drugs with him and after three months it dawned on me what was happening. I was rapidly building up a tolerance for the drugs and they were beginning to lose effect. They weren't taking away the pain any more. I wondered why Seán put up with me when all I could do was cry. I couldn't tell him why I was crying and he never pushed me to talk about it. He just let me curl up into a ball and sob my heart out for weeks on end. I was grateful for his support. He told me that it was alright for me to cry as he gently rubbed my shoulder and reminded me that I was going to be ok. I really wasn't that sure. The world didn't have much to offer me any more.

Chapter 15 ∾

| TWO STEPS BACK

It was 2005 and almost two years had passed since my relapse, following my bust-up with Justin. By now I was spiritually bankrupt and mentally warped, with the emotional capacity of the thirteen-year-old I had been when I had first started using drugs. I made a promise to myself that I would never again make the effort to stop using drugs. My relapses only added to my self-defeating thoughts and for the first time in my life I truly accepted that I would die a hopeless drug addict. This was a huge relief. The fight to get clean was over and I could selfishly get on with passively committing suicide.

My family knew that it was only a matter of time before I died. They left me to it in the knowledge that they had done all they could do for me. All of them except for my mother. She was trying to make a life for herself and Philip in Lanzarote. We hardly ever spoke now, as we were both riddled with our own guilt about never having the courage to be honest with each other. While my mother was away, I moved into her apartment in the city centre with my two friends Seán and Neil, the only two people on the planet that I could trust. We took turns shop-lifting to feed our habits, but most days I was too ill to move. The drugs had stunted my growth and I had lost the power of my left arm from injecting into an artery; many of my veins in my arms had collapsed or had thrombosis. Neil and Seán could get a hit of heroin without much hassle, but sometimes I would spend up to thirteen hours desperately trying to get the heroin into me. At stages I sadistically found this ritual pleasurable. It made me feel alive and it gave me something to take my mind off my real pain.

My obsession with hurting myself started off with a wound on my forearm. I began savagely to inject the heroin directly into the wound. As soon as I could see the blood entering the barrel, then surely I was getting some sort of a hit. Within a few months the wound extended from my elbow right down to my wrist. So I began to chip away at my other arm. Then I worked my way onto both of my hands. After a while, butchering myself became the norm and Neil and Seán learned to keep their mouths shut and to just keep an eye on me. My tolerance for drugs had decreased because I couldn't get enough drugs into me and I spent more times sick than stoned. Most days when I managed to successfully get the heroin into me, I would overdose, leaving myself badly bruised from falls. This also became the norm and Seán quickly learned how to snap me out of it. Once I didn't turn blue, I would be ok. I spent a lot of my time in and out of hospital due to the infections in my arms.

Another year passed and in 2006 my doctor gave me a serious warning that if I didn't stop using drugs, they would have to amputate both of my arms. I was watching my arms rot away right before my eyes. The heroin seemed to be eating them alive.

It was during this time that my whole universe shifted. I realised that the drugs had stopped working a long time earlier, possibly when I had come back from Italy. Somewhere along the line, whether it was the praying, or the NA meetings, or the rehab in the Rutland Centre, a seed had been planted and I had found my conscience. Now it was just impossible for me to use drugs in peace. I had tried everything in an attempt to block it all out: running from country to country trying to put oceans between myself and my addiction, getting involved with madmen to distract me from my own madness, hiding behind bullshit, lies and make-believe identities to give my ego a nice boost, using my illness as an excuse to cop out of life and to abandon any responsibility that might hinder my drug use, convincing myself that I didn't care less whether I lived or died.

I continued to butcher myself, but as I did so my mind fine-combed through my life. Piecing it all together like a jigsaw. I thought of my sponsor Katriona and the knowledge that she had tried to pass on to me. 'Why can't I stay clean?' I had asked her one day shortly after my relapse in 2004.

'Rachael, the solution to staying clean is so simple that you miss it every time.' Here it was, I'd thought, Katriona was going to tell me something so profound that it would completely blow me away and change my life forever.

'What is it?' I'd asked her in anticipation.

'You can't stay clean, Rachael, because you keep on using drugs,' she had said calmly.

I had been baffled. 'What, that's it? End of story?'

'Yeah, when it comes to the crunch, it's as simple as that.'

'But it couldn't be, Katriona. It can't be that easy. Sure if that was the case, I would have got clean years ago.'

'Well, there comes a point in your life when you just have to let go of the past and stop using it as an excuse to continue to use drugs. And when you do that, it *is* that simple.'

'And how do I let go of the past then?' I'd asked her.

'You ask God to help you to let go and you pray for the people who have hurt you.'

I had felt extremely frustrated when Katriona told me this. '*Me*, pray for the people who have hurt me?! Why should I pray for them: they don't deserve it.'

'I understand what you're saying, Rachael, but maybe *you* deserve it. Because as long as you hold onto that hurt, you'll never have any freedom.'

I didn't know it at the time, but she had hit a huge nerve with me. For three years I tried to make sense of what Katriona had told me. I couldn't get her voice out of my head. I thought about our conversations over and over again. I had to let go because *I* deserved it? She had asked me one day if my expectations of people, particularly of my mother, were reasonable. I thought that they were. She *was* my mother, after all, and she ought to act like one. Then Katriona had asked me what it was about my mother that threatened me so deeply.

At that time the thought of even answering that question pushed me over the edge. But now I could no longer deny the truth. I had what recovering alcoholics call 'a moment of clarity'. Holy shit, I thought, I *was* holding on to the past and using it as an excuse to keep using drugs. By replaying in my head the hurt that others had done to me, I was actually hurting myself. And where were *they* all now? Getting on with their lives, that's where! More than likely completely oblivious to the power that I was giving them. And why was I so threatened by my mother? I wondered. The answer to this question lay at the core of why I used drugs in the first place. If my own mother couldn't love me, then who would and how on earth could I? Deep down I believed that I was just unlovable.

For so many years I had been in awe of my mother. She was everything that I ever wanted to be. She was beautiful and glamorous and loved by anyone with whom she came in contact. She seemed to touch everyone's lives except mine. What she did and what she said was gospel and I felt ugly and inadequate in comparison to her. I began to allow myself to think that maybe my expectations of her as a mother weren't that reasonable after all. I thought about her life and realised the resemblance that it bore to mine. We were so similar when I thought about it. How could she possibly show me any love when she hadn't received any herself? She had been ruled by three men in her life: my grandfather, my father and Philip's father and each and every one of them had abused her in some form or another. My mother could never love me in the way that I wanted her to until, that was, she learned to love herself. And in return, I could never accept her love or anyone else's until *I* learned to love myself. And there it was, I had found my solution. I needed to find a way to truly love myself.

It all sounded brilliant in theory but it nearly killed me to get my head around this concept. In order for me to learn to love myself, I would have to let go of a lot of old hurts. Easier said than done. But death was a reality for me now. And I was no longer afraid. I knew that before I did anything, I needed to get clean first. I was ready to give recovery one last shot.

———

Somebody once told me that the easy part of recovering from addiction is getting clean, and the hard part is *staying* clean. But I have never once come across a hardcore drug addict who says that it is easy to get clean. I had made many mistakes in the past, but the one thing I had learned was that I couldn't do it on my own. 'Get humble or be humiliated,' I was told by countless recovering drug addicts. 'You can't save your face and your arse at the same time,' one had said. At the time I had cringed and sniggered to myself at their corny clichés, but now that my life depended on it and I was actually eating humble pie, I was finally beginning to understand what they had meant. It wasn't about the clichés. It was about the positive attitude behind them and a willingness to do whatever it took to get clean and to stay clean.

I knew that I couldn't set myself up for failure by going through cold-turkey, only to realise that, halfway through it, the pain was too much for me to handle. Then I would end up using drugs and completely lose heart. Staying on methadone wasn't an option for me either. I just wasn't a great believer in the stuff. Fair enough if people were happy to stay on it for the rest of their lives and they used it to give them some sort of normality, but in my experience complete abstinence from drugs was the only way forward. I knew I had to be careful. I had learned the hard way about the power and the sneakiness of my addiction, that part of me that was ever present, always one step ahead of me, just waiting for me to be weak so that it could fill me with delusional thoughts and negativity.

——

My desire to stop using drugs was born once again. Now all I had to do was to find a way to do it. Timing was everything. If I didn't stop using drugs, my arms would have to be amputated. I needed the support of a detox centre. Even though I had great admiration for many of my friends who had stopped using drugs with the support of Narcotics Anonymous, I knew in my heart that this wasn't for me. I would have to be hospitalised in a safe environment. But everywhere I went, there were endless waiting lists. Anyone I spoke to simply passed the buck to somebody else. I was frustrated and full of despair and for the first time in years I got down on my knees and with all my heart I asked God to help me. I even asked Big Mick for a dig-out. I was ready to surrender to God and to anyone else who cared to help me.

Then one day my mother rang me out of the blue. She told me that she and Philip had made the decision to come home. My grandmother had told them that it wouldn't be long before I was dead. She was now in Dublin and she wanted to talk to me. Ah no, I thought. What did she want? What was she going to say to me? I hadn't expected this to happen.

Myself and Seán were in her apartment when she arrived with my aunt Jacqueline. She was still as beautiful as ever and she didn't seem fazed by Seán or the mess in her apartment. In fact she was as cool as a cucumber, although I knew by her that this was an act. I was just waiting for the shit to hit the fan. But she couldn't seem to muster up the courage to say what she needed to say.

She and Jacqueline went out for a few drinks and Jacqueline returned to the flat alone. Even though I was used to my mother glossing over things, I was really gutted that she had said nothing, not even now. Jacqueline, on the other hand, was in a seriously bad mood and began to get on Seán's case. 'Why are you even in this flat?' she said to him. She kept at him. On and on, calling him names and trying to humiliate him. I don't know what came over me. I had never in all of my life, even at the worst of times, raised my hand to any family members. I was never a fighter and I made it my business to keep away from violence. But in that moment everything came to the surface and I couldn't control myself. I gave Jacqueline a merciless whack with the back of my hand. I hit her nose and within seconds it was gushing blood.

The reality of what I had done kicked in straight away. 'Oh my God,' Jacqueline screamed, 'I can't believe you did that. How could you do that to me?'

I felt guilty and I immediately ran to where she stood. 'Jacqueline, I'm so sorry I didn't mean it.' With her hand to her nose she stormed past me into the sitting-room and she rang my mother. Then *I* rang my mother, crying hysterically, trying to tell her what had happened and how sorry I was.

About ten minutes later I saw Philip looking through the kitchen window from outside. It must have looked like a murder scene from where he stood—the kitchen was full of blood. Within minutes Philip had smashed the front door window in and he was charging at me like a lunatic. 'Why are you doing this to us?' he shouted, throwing punches into the air. My mother and Jacqueline held him back, but he looked as though he didn't know whether to hold me or to hit me. Then he broke down crying and my mother began to get upset.

She pulled me up off the floor and she tore my cardigan off, revealing my arms. 'Look what you're doing to yourself,' she shrilled, holding me by the wrists. 'Look at your fucking arms, Rachael. Look at them.'

'I know what they look like, ma.'

'You mustn't! Do you even realise what you're doing to yourself? Do you realise what you're doing to us?' she screamed. 'Do you hate yourself that much that you would do this to yourself? Do you hate *me* that much that you would do this to yourself?' She had held everything back for years. Now it was all coming out and she was sobbing. 'I know that I haven't been there for you, Rachael. Every day of my life, I have to live with that guilt. And I'm sorry. I'm so sorry. If I could turn back the clock, I would do everything differently. I wouldn't send you to Cuba or even to Texas. I would be there for you and you'll never know how sorry I am. I've tried to move on with my own life. But I'll *never* be happy until I know that you're happy. But I'm here now, Rachael. Look at me!' she screamed, shaking my skinny frame. 'I'm here now.' She tightly wrapped her arms around me. 'I'm here now.'

That was the first moment that I realised just how my addiction was affecting my family. All of my life everything had been about me. *My* pain, *my* hurt, *my* loneliness, *my* innocence. Pointing the finger at pretty much anyone who came across my path and who didn't behave in the way that I wanted them to. The whole world had it in for me and I had no comprehension of anyone else's troubles except my own. But something had changed within me over the previous weeks. I knew now that *I* was the problem and that only *I* could change things. This was my final turning point.

Chapter 16 ∽

| A NEW BEGINNING

After my arrest for shop-lifting with Neil, my escape from Pearse Street and all the media frenzy that followed, I ended up right where I had started as an addict—in prison. But this time, for a different reason. This time, I was going to prison because I had committed a crime, sure, but also because I knew that prison would keep me away from drugs and give me the start I needed on the road to getting clean for good.

After my arrest for shop-lifting in July 2006 I arrived in the Dóchas Women's Centre at about 9:30 p.m. and I was quickly strip-searched, showered and sent to the medical unit where I received a set of old pyjamas, old sheets and a duvet cover, a toothbrush and toothpaste, a miniature box of Cornflakes and a carton of milk. After being informed that I would see the doctor the next day, I was sent to a transitional two-person cell that was already occupied by a young girl from Bosnia. She was a striking looking girl with long blonde hair, milky skin and big sad eyes that told a story of hardship. She smiled at me as I entered the cell, looking exactly how I felt, frightened and vulnerable.

That night Maria told me all about her country and her family. I felt sorry for her, but I was also thankful to her because she distracted me from my withdrawals, which were getting worse by the minute. It was a long sleepless night of tossing and turning, battling with my own mind and trying my best not to torment myself by thinking about drugs. The next day myself and Maria were moved over to the real part of the prison. It was state of the art—six different houses with names like Maple, Hazel and Laurel. The houses were designed to segregate the prisoners from each other, depending on their situation and type of sentence. I was brought to Maple, which accommodated sixteen women, most of them drug addicts just like myself. They were in custody on various different charges, like me and were waiting to be dealt with by the courts. We had a communal kitchen, which appeared to be immaculate, and a sitting-room complete with a plasma TV. Our cells were not unlike bedrooms, with portable televisions and en-suite showers and toilets. Apart from not being allowed into other prisoners' houses, we could come and go as we pleased within the grounds of Dóchas. It was a far cry from the old women's prison, Mountjoy, which was cockroach-infested and overcrowded. The only thing that had not changed was the women who were imprisoned there. I knew most of them from Mountjoy and I was surprised that half of them were still alive.

After a long wait to be assessed by the doctor, I received my ninety mls of methadone. It was such a relief to feel my bones and my blood warm up, but this only took away the pains and helped me to function just enough to protect myself from the other women in Dóchas. There were many young girls trying to make a reputation and a name for themselves who were loud and boisterous. They would take any opportunity to humiliate you in front of others. By nature I wasn't a fighter and at this stage in my life I hadn't the energy to pretend that I was. All I could do was be myself and hope that knowing most of the old-timers would guarantee me some element of safety.

I quickly settled into my cell and established a routine of doing nothing. There were many activities that a prisoner could get involved in, such as going to school, getting lessons in hair and beauty or going to the fully equipped gym for a class in aerobics. But all I wanted to do was lock myself into my cell. Even though drugs were readily available beyond my four walls—and sometimes within them—I realised that being locked up was a chance to get myself off the heroin. I knew that this would be far from easy, but I made a decision to do my best.

It wasn't helped by the fact that the days at Dóchas were long and boring. The highlight of my day was getting my methadone and wishing my time away. I knew that spending too much time on my own wasn't a good idea, because I had too much time to think. For the time to go quickly, I needed to be around the other prisoners. It was July and the sun was blazing in the sky, so myself and some other girls would sit in the garden. Some of them would tell me all about their lives and how they ended up in prison. Most of the girls I spoke to lived lives that were full of regret and guilt. Others hadn't an ounce of remorse and got great pleasure in telling me all about the crimes they had committed.

One girl in particular, who was much younger than me and whom I had known since she was a little kid, insisted on telling me in graphic detail about the murder she had committed. She had already been convicted and was looking at spending the foreseeable future in prison. We both sat alone in her cell as she animatedly told me her story. As I listened to this young, pretty girl, I thought to myself, Jesus, what happened to you. I was dizzy, I felt like vomiting and the hairs on my arms stood up with fright. I knew this girl looked up to me and she was trying to impress me. I couldn't get out of her cell quickly enough. There but for the grace of God, I thought. I may not have murdered anyone, but I had done plenty of other bad things.

Sometimes I would sit and watch the girls get their drugs in. It baffled me how the prison officers wouldn't even notice what the women were up to: they must have been blind. The women would congregate by the prison wall waiting for their 'dropsy' to be thrown over. All of a sudden, I would see a package flying over the wall. Then the women would scatter and one of them would stay behind, suspiciously looking around for her deal. This is how most of the arguments would start in prison. The women would take turns 'sorting each other out' with their drugs. Most of the time somebody would get left out or ripped off. This would lead to huge fights, with some pulling others down flights of stairs by the hair and even scalding each other with boiling water mixed with sugar. The ironic thing is that the Dóchas Centre had no facilities to help those of us who might have wanted to become drug-free. There were no counsellors to talk to or groups that would be of any benefit to us. The problem of drugs was being avoided, which defeated the purpose of any sort of rehabilitation.

I kept my head down and tried to stay focused. My court day was slowly approaching and I was certain that a bed would become available.

One morning my cell door was unlocked and my fluorescent lights were turned on. 'Rachael, it's time to get up, pack your stuff and be ready in twenty minutes.' I was relieved and ready to say goodbye to Dóchas Prison. After packing all my belongings, I was given my methadone and brought to court. Once again I was put in a grotty little cell. I sat alone and prayed that the judge was in a good mood. My destiny lay in his hands. Staying clean for one week in prison was difficult enough. Anything more than that just seemed impossible. Please God, let there be a bed available, I thought as I stood to meet my fate in front of Judge Cormac Dunne.

'Well, Ms Keogh, a week in prison has obviously done you the world of good. You look a lot better,' the judge stated. 'What is the situation with Cuan Dara?' he addressed my solicitor.

'Your honour, we have been in close contact with Cuan Dara, but due to the waiting list, a bed has not become available as yet.' My heart sank. 'They have informed us that the next bed that becomes available will be for Rachael, but that could take anything up to six weeks. I would, however, ask the court to take into consideration Ms Keogh's circumstances. She is a young woman who has battled serious drug addiction for a number of years. She has had long periods of being completely drug-free and she says that she realises where she went wrong. She believes that if she is given the chance, she could become drug-free again, but she and her family maintain that going back to prison could be detrimental to any chance that she has in achieving this.'

'Really? Where is her family?'

'Her mother is with us in court today.'

'Where are you, Mrs Keogh? Mrs Keogh, would you please come up here and tell us what you think?' the judge requested. I was beginning to feel nauseous, but I knew that my mother would speak up for me. I heard shuffling sounds coming from behind me, then the echoing noise of my mother's footsteps as she walked past me, up to her designated seat.

'Well, Mrs Keogh, do you think that going back to prison would jeopardise Rachael's chance of recovery?' the judge asked. Everyone looked at my mother and waited for her to respond. She said nothing. She sat silent and frozen to the spot. Tell them what you think ma, tell them, I screamed in my head, hoping that somehow she would hear me.

'Mrs Keogh?' the judge said, urging her to respond.

Then my mother's bottom lip began to wobble and I knew that she was about to cry. No, no, don't cry, don't cry, I thought, but my mother broke down and sobbed her heart out in front of the whole court.

'Ok, Mrs Keogh, thank you very much. You may step down now,' said the judge with a hint of sympathy in his voice. Then he turned and looked at me as if to say, 'Shame on you for putting your poor mother through this.' He shook his head and sighed heavily, addressing my solicitor. 'Mrs Brennan, I have no choice but to put your client back into custody until I know for certain that what you are saying is true. I will hand this case over to the recommendation of Dr Brian Sweeney. He will assess Ms Keogh in the Dóchas Women's Centre during next week. Next court date, one week from now.'

I was devastated to be back in prison. It really felt like I was back at square one in my recovery, but strangely enough, things turned out quite differently. Perhaps it was Dr Sweeney's quiet listening to my family story and the chance to pour out my heart to him and not be judged, that made me realise I could do this, I *could* get clean. After telling Dr Sweeney everything during my second trip to Dóchas, it seemed that the worst was over. I even surprised myself by not using heroin while I was in prison. With the knowledge that I had been freely given from Narcotics Anonymous, I decided to take things one day at a time, or if needs be, one second at a time. I asked God to help me and it worked.

I was granted bail pending a place becoming available at Cuan Dara, on condition that I attend NA meetings. I was free. But I was still on ninety mls of methadone and I needed to stick with my plan and my bail conditions. If I did this, my doctor agreed to reduce my dose to forty mls of methadone and make me a priority for Cuan Dara detox centre. Keeping busy was a must, so I went to three and four NA meetings a day, surrounding myself with people who had gone before me. Whether I knew them or even liked them, it didn't matter. Once I was with other recovering drug addicts, I knew that I wouldn't use drugs.

Most days I got great relief from the meetings. I was in a place where people understood me. There were no authority figures or people threatening to throw me out because I was still on methadone. I was told by many that I had earned my chair and that I was to 'keep coming back'. Other days I hung on by the 'skin of my teeth', but I did my best to listen and to take advice. 'Do the opposite to what your head tells you,' I was told. 'If you feel like using drugs, come to a meeting and tell somebody. Bring the body and the mind will follow.' I used the clichés as my mantra. All that mattered to me now was that I keep moving forward. And as the days passed by, I became stronger and more determined than *ever* before.

———

Six weeks had passed and I had abided by my bail conditions. But there was still no sign of an available bed in Cuan Dara. My mother had meant what she had said. She was standing by my side in everything that I did, encouraging me to persevere and to have faith. Both of us knew that a lot of damage had been done between the two of us and we would have a lot of talking to do if we wanted to get on with each other, but now wasn't the time to think about it. Every day she helped me to dress and bandage my arms. They no longer had gaping wounds on them and it seemed that they were beginning to heal well.

In my desperation to get clean I exposed myself to the media and to the public. It was a last resort to get help for my addiction, but to my astonishment my story exploded onto every newspaper across the country and kept popping up in the following months. I had to keep my two feet firmly on the ground and remember what I had done it all for, to get clean; not to get carried away with the little bit of fame and recognition that I was receiving. My life was at stake and I had to remember who I was and where I wanted to go.

Three months had passed now and my frustration was growing over the lack of available beds in any suitable detox unit. And when Sky News asked me if they could make a fly-on-the-wall documentary about my journey through recovery, to follow up on their original story about my addiction, I agreed. Someone once told me that desperation was 'a gift'. A gift that gives you the ability to run through brick walls. I had that gift now. I had been to hell and back and if I could get through all that, I could get through absolutely anything. All of a sudden I had a great confidence and an enthusiasm that I had never possessed before. I was no longer afraid to face up to myself or anyone else for that matter. I wasn't going to play a role that others had chosen for me any more. I would be myself, rotten arms and all, and if you didn't like me, then you could 'Kiss my arse'.

Sky News used me for a good story and I used them to show

people the reality of addiction and the third-world facilities that we have in Ireland for people who were seeking treatment. I had now been waiting for four months to go into Cuan Dara and I still hadn't used heroin. I was doing everything that I could possibly think of to push my case forward. Becoming an annoyance to anyone who had the power to help me, even storming Dáil Éireann and confronting the minister responsible for the government's drug strategy. Why was I waiting this long? I demanded to know. I was going to lose both my arms if I didn't receive help. The minister, who was sitting on a panel with his fellow politicians, had a look of puzzlement on his face, and beads of sweat ran down his forehead. He didn't reply to my question.

———

The drugs had taken their toll on my health. My body was still very weak and I spent my twenty-eighth birthday in hospital. At first the doctors thought that I had tuberculosis, but I was later to learn that I had residual heroin attached to my lungs. This blockage and lack of oxygen resulted in bad circulation and clubbing of my fingers. I also learned that I had hepatitis C. But this only made me more determined to become drug-free. Two days after my birthday a bed became available for me in Cuan Dara. I thought that I couldn't get there quick enough and as soon as I arrived I broke down, crying with relief. I had made it. The nightmare was over now. I knew exactly what to expect this time and I knew exactly what I had to do. And come hell or high water, I would stick it out.

After six days of being weaned off methadone, I was completely drug-free and for six weeks after that I crawled the walls, suffering with the usual aches and pains and insomnia. I cried my heart out and laughed my head off, but mostly I was full of anger and rage. I was adamant that people treat me with respect and I wasn't letting anyone away with anything. I would no longer say 'yes' when I meant 'no'. Almost everyone got an earful off me. My counsellor, my doctor, even some of the other clients. If anyone attempted to try and drag me down, I was ready physically to harm them. I was fighting for my life here. I exhausted every facility that was on offer. Every bit of energy that I had channelled into my drug addiction was now being channelled into my recovery.

When my six weeks of detox ended in Cuan Dara I was offered a place in a rehabilitation centre called Keltoi. I was clean now and I had already done work on myself in Cuan Dara and was in danger of being complacent. What did I need with another rehab? I was sorted, I thought. I had broken the hold heroin had on me and had promised myself I'd never look back. Then I was reminded by my good friend Declan, whom I had met in NA, that this was my addiction talking, speaking to me in my own voice and convincing me that I was sorted. After talking to Declan, I realised that I was actually terrified of going back into rehab: I wasn't sure I could face further confrontation with myself and others, more First Steps and constant questioning of my motives. But Declan encouraged me to persist, telling me that the longest journey I would ever make would be the journey from my head to my heart. Going into Keltoi would be the beginning of that journey. I felt as though I were jumping off a cliff.

Declan had surprised me throughout my relapse. I had ducked and dived from NA members all through it, but for some reason I kept bumping into him. I knew that my relapse had affected him deeply, but he'd managed to stay clean. Every time I saw him when I was using, he offered to help me. He believed in me when I didn't believe in myself. My relapse taught me who my real friends were and I knew that Declan was one of them. It was karma that Declan should be with me now.

Keltoi means 'the hidden people,' and is neatly tucked away in the largest park in Ireland. It didn't look anything like a treatment centre to me. It was a three-storey yellow building that looked more like a modern respite home. Keltoi took in eight clients over the space of eight weeks, which created an intimacy between the staff and clients, and on my first day in Keltoi I was introduced to everyone including the dog. Most of the clients I already knew from Narcotics Anonymous, which made me feel more at ease. There were seven of us in total, five men and a girl with whom had I been through Cuan Dara.

I felt as though I were walking into the Little House on the Prairie. Everything seemed so peaceful and harmonious, right down to the deer who happily nibbled on the grass and lounged around in the garden. I was used to the confrontational approach of therapy, where I was vigilantly observed by staff and clients alike and ruthlessly made aware of my character defects. Keltoi was something completely different. Clients were expected to find their own answers within themselves. The six counsellors on site were there to gently challenge us and nudge us in the right direction.

I had been half expecting somebody to jump out at me and frog-march me into group therapy, where I would be torn apart for being such a bold girl. But that never happened. Everyone was warm and friendly, to the point where I was starting to think that it was all a set-up. I wasn't used to people being so nice to me without looking for something in return. There were lots of surprises at Keltoi. When dinner time came, two of the staff sat down at the table to eat with the clients. This was a first. Usually in treatment centres the staff eat their meals in a separate room, but I was told that nobody was above or below anybody else in Keltoi. Everything that the clients did, the staff did. We worked together and we ate together. There was no 'us' and 'them'.

The daily routine was laid-back but structured. Breakfast began at ten and we weren't allowed to eat until everyone was at the breakfast table. Then we would all sit around together and go over our plan for the day. Each of us had a duty to carry out, whether it was working in the kitchen preparing home-made meals from scratch, or cleaning the house. We were kept occupied from ten o'clock in the morning until lunchtime. When we were finished our lunch we had free time until two o'clock. This was when group therapy took place.

At my first day in group I was told to introduce myself and to sit back and take in how the group worked. I couldn't believe it. The conversation was light on the head and it focused on the here and the now. There was no 'deep-sea diving' into the past. It was suggested that unless we really needed to share something of a delicate nature, we could hold onto it until we had our one-to-one session with a counsellor of our choice. But seeing a counsellor needed to be planned one week in advance, so I immediately put in a request to see each and every one of them. Group therapy ended at around three-thirty. Then we were free until six o'clock when we had our tea. At seven-thirty we had a wind-down group, taking twenty minutes to reflect on the highs and lows of our day. After wind-down we were free to watch television or just hang out together until it was time to go to bed.

And that was it. That was Keltoi in a bag. I had never experienced anything like it in my life. Used to guessing what others wanted of me in treatment and giving it to them, I found Keltoi a shock to begin with. No-one gave me orders or showed me what to do, nobody told me what they were thinking. And I *really* needed to know what everyone was thinking. That way I would know where I stood. But it wasn't a game. It appeared to be the most 'normal' treatment centre I had ever come across. I was later to learn that Keltoi was designed that way on purpose: being left to our own devices in a safe place would teach us self-reliance and self-trust. And after two weeks I began to really feel at home.

I had never been one for hanging out with the girls. My experiences in prison had turned me off them and, in spite of everything I had gone through with men, I had always felt more comfortable with them. But things had changed with me this time. I planned to stay as far away from men as possible and to start making friendships with women as Katriona, my NA sponsor, had advised me. This would be difficult for me. I couldn't manipulate women. They would see right through me. But then I remembered that I no longer had the need to manipulate anyone. I had nothing to hide and people's opinions of me didn't matter any more.

Rachel and I didn't see eye to eye at first, in spite of sharing the same name. She had come into Cuan Dara two weeks after me. She was the same age and she had the same taste in clothes. We should have had a lot in common, but I had no idea how to approach her. We tried to be polite to each other, but we avoided being left alone together at all costs. I knew that we had to clear the air, but I had no idea what I would say to her. So I decided to just be honest. We both sat alone together and I told Rachel how much I admired her for sticking with the detox and coming into rehab, as it was her first time. It had taken me ten years to get this far. She then told me how much she admired me and had secretly done so, even in Cuan Dara. But her fear of women had got the better of her.

The more that I spoke to Rachel, the more I realised how much we had in common. We both loved dancing, music and singing. After that initial chat, we became firm friends, so much so that within two weeks, the other clients were jokingly accusing myself and Rachel of being co-dependent. (That's how rehab is. You enter with one addiction and all of a sudden you have dozens of them!) But the counsellors encouraged our friendship: we had missed out on so many years of doing girlie things and Keltoi gave us the freedom to make up for lost time.

Rachel and I spent most of our free time together, telling each other our innermost secrets, heartily laughing together about embarrassing things that we had done in our addiction and at times crying together with the sheer relief of being clean and having each other to share it with. Any chance we got, we made up dances, chatted about fashion and defended each other in group therapy. I was learning all over again what it meant to have a girlfriend and to be a girlfriend.

———

My time in Keltoi would be over in the blink of an eye and I planned to make the best of it. I had learned so much about myself and my addiction over the years and my relapses hadn't taken that away from me. I had no question in my mind or any doubt about whether or not I was an addict. No matter what I did, I couldn't use *any* mood-altering substance without it having devastating consequences. I truly accepted this now without any reservation. My addiction was intricately part of my make-up. If I really wanted to recover I would have to change *everything*: my thinking, my behaviour, my perception of myself *and* of the world around me. Day by day I would have to learn how to live with that. Keltoi was teaching me how to put into practice all that I had learned.

My new-found ability to do things that had been beyond my control in the past made me question my belief in a power greater than myself. Did I even believe in God any more, or was I the one who was doing all the work and not God? I couldn't deny the fact that I had escaped death on more than one occasion. Was that just luck or coincidental? Was I making things harder for myself by believing in God, or had I *really* been carried through my addiction by a higher power? If I was, why me? Why had so many of my friends died and not me? I wasn't sure. But I had always been certain of the fact that when I meditated and I stilled my mind I was no longer tormented by my addiction. I somehow found a strength which surpassed my own capabilities.

But the whole God thing had got me into trouble before, and so now it was important for me to take serious stock of my beliefs around all of this. And I came to the realisation that any suffering I had encountered had absolutely nothing to do with God. The God of my understanding wasn't a judgmental tyrant who sat on a cloud setting up ways for me to fall flat on my face and to suffer unnecessarily. I really didn't know what 'God' was, but it was something that was inside of me and all around me. It was an energy that was loving and caring, forgiving and understanding. It was there for me to tap into whenever I wanted.

I had always been too afraid to truly get in touch with this good side of myself before. It wasn't familiar and I didn't trust it. If I got in touch with this side of myself, my heart would surely crumble. I would become too soft and people would take me for an eegit. So I held on to the negativity and I fed it. This was my way of keeping some sort of control. But look where it had got me. All that bullshit was over now. I intended to do things differently. In the quietness of meditation, I was recognising the difference between my addiction and myself as a human being. It was all very simple now. My addiction was negative and *I* was positive. I was learning how to nourish my positive side. I had been told to give myself positive affirmations—even if I didn't believe what I was saying I would do it anyway. I found that, over time, this technique was really beginning to work for me.

Apart from the spiritual side, Keltoi put a lot of emphasis on practicalities. The importance of planning out my day and sticking with my plan. I had no concept of time or planning. My attitude had been that somehow, someway, everything would magically fall into place and without any effort on my behalf. With the help of the clients and the staff in Keltoi, I realised that this type of attitude had always got me into trouble. It was one of the many things that I needed to change. So I began to make a real effort to get out of bed on time. To be at the breakfast table on time. To do my job on time. And in doing these simple things I began to feel like a human being again. I was learning the meaning of self-discipline and achievement. And my failure to do these simple things had always marked the beginning of my past relapses into drug addiction.

I was halfway through my rehabilitation and I was loving every minute of it. But, for me, letting go of the drugs was as though someone had died. I felt as though I was grieving and becoming liberated all at once. The camaraderie that I shared with the other clients got me through the tough times. And I knew that I was blessed to be around such a wonderful bunch of people.

I kept pictures on my wall of Justin and some other people who had hurt me in the past. As strange as it may seem, they were my driving force at times. The pictures empowered me, reminding me that it wasn't what they had done to me that played a part in me going back using drugs; it was how I had reacted to what they had done to me that caused me the most pain. I now knew in my heart that nobody could really hurt me any more than I could hurt myself. And I would never again give anyone that power. Not Justin, Derek, any man or woman, or even my family. It was my responsibility now who I let into my life. And I had learned the hard way that not everyone could be trusted. I wouldn't wear my heart on my sleeve the way I had done before: people would have to earn my trust.

During this time, my family came to visit me, but when *I* let them. For so many years I had been emotionally enmeshed with them, destroying myself because they couldn't be the people that I wanted them to be. Praying for them was helping me to accept them for who they were and I was slowly but surely realising that they had done their best with what they had. I was still terribly angry and hurt though. It would probably take me the rest of my life to heal from everything that had happened, but I had stopped trying to understand why I ended up the way I did. I stopped trying to understand my addiction and I stopped trying to understand God. It was pointless because they were things that were beyond my comprehension. Anyway, I couldn't live my life and stay clean on knowledge alone. The solution for me now was accepting that I was an addict. Having faith that I was being looked after in a spiritual sense. Being true to myself and simply trying to do the next right thing. Keltoi had been just what I needed.

After all that peace and quiet, that meditation and reflection, I was dreading leaving Keltoi in some ways. Would the media and the public exposure be too much for me to handle? Did I really want to be known as 'the girl with the arms' or 'the face of heroin'? All I wanted was to get clean. I was just one of thousands of recovering addicts all over the world. The only difference between me and them was that I had made my story known to the public. Yes, it was a miracle that I had got clean and I definitely had a story to tell. But I had to stay grounded and not get carried away with the glory of it all.

Keltoi had arranged living accommodation for me in transitional housing for when I left, in what is called a 'step-down' programme, which provides support and counselling in a centre in Dublin city. The accommodation was a one-bedroomed apartment and it was ideal. I had my NA meetings within arm's reach and Keltoi provided one-to-one counselling sessions and after-care weekly for that extra bit of support. I was delighted when my friend Rachel got a place on the same programme. By now we were inseparable. Other close friends were offered transitional housing not too far away. One of the conditions of my stay in transitional housing was that I attend a day programme, preferably of a rehabilitative nature. I point-blank refused. I would do a day programme but I wanted to move away from rehabilitation: I had done all that before and now it was time for a change. My goal was to go to college at some stage and I knew that I needed to prepare myself. So we came to the agreement that I would do an educational day programme. And this suited me fine.

Chapter 17 ∿

| LETTING GO

I was set up in my new life, with all the support I needed, but I also had another reason to look forward to the future.

Patrick had come to Keltoi when I had settled in and had just got comfortable in my skin. One Tuesday, the buzz went around that a new client was arriving. I tried to not pay attention. I was in Keltoi to focus on myself, and the last thing that I needed was a distraction. When the new client arrived I was doing my household chores. I knew his face to see. I had seen him around town, but I had never spoken to him before. It was his glittering blue eyes that had stuck in my head. He politely shook my hand and he introduced himself as Patrick. Just by his appearance I knew that he came from a good family. (When an addict has a good family, it makes the world of difference to his/her health and well-being.) Patrick was a little bit taller than myself, slender but well built. His hair was dark with a trendy cut to it. I tried not to notice how attractive he was, but when he picked up the guitar and he began to sing during our free time, I found myself drooling.

It wasn't in my character to drool. The only time I had drooled was when I was goofing off on heroin, but of all the people who I had met during my life, none of them made my heart skip a beat like he did. Talk about seeing sparks. I couldn't take my eyes off him. I had to pinch myself and remind myself why I was in Keltoi. Don't go there, I told myself. Relationships always get you into trouble. I had fought so hard to get this far and I wasn't about to jeopardise myself or anyone else just for some sort of instant gratification, or to feel good about myself. Been there, done that.

Thank God for the no-physical-contact rule, I thought. Of course the more I got to know Patrick, the more I fancied him. But I was in early recovery, my hormones were all over the place and I just didn't trust myself yet. I couldn't keep this to myself, so I decided to tell one of the counsellors. 'You know, your secrets grow in the dark, so you did the right thing by being honest,' said the counsellor. Now that the counsellors knew, I definitely couldn't act on my desires. And I knew that the counsellors would keep an eye on us both.

I couldn't stop thinking about Patrick though. I found myself completely in awe of him. Everything about him made me spin. He was gorgeous, talented, musically gifted, well-educated, a great listener and really funny. When he told me that he was attracted to me, I felt like a little girl again. But I didn't let him know that. Then he said that he respected me too much to even try anything on with me. Not that I would have let him. But I liked that he had his priorities straight. He was in the same boat as me and he wasn't about to mess up.

So it was out in the open for everyone to see. I was human after all, with the same needs as everyone else, but I was conscious of the fact that I had a big part to play in the disastrous relationships that I had had in the past. I wasn't totally innocent in it all. I had always been attracted to men who were bad boys and who wouldn't treat me right. I wasn't about to make the same mistake again.

Myself and Patrick were reminded to focus on our recovery— there were to be no exclusive relationships in Keltoi. Some days I couldn't stay in the same room as him. He was too much of a distraction. Working in the kitchen together was sheer torture. We would be accompanied by one of the counsellors, but I couldn't see anyone but him. We kept our distance from each other as he sang to me from the other side of the kitchen. He called me his

Golden Barley. Sometimes I would ask him to help me just so that I could be close to him. He would happily oblige.

I decided that I was going to marry Patrick some day and have his babies with him when the time was right. Rachel thought that this was funny. 'Ah, yeah, typical addict. You hardly even know him and you have your life planned out with him already.' But I had never experienced anything like this before. I never felt for anyone the way I did about him.

Everyone knew that myself and Patrick were mad about each other. The chemistry between us was explosive. I was truly tested and challenged around my attraction for him in Keltoi, but we both managed to be as honest as we could without breaking any of the rules. The difficulty would be when we got out, and I knew in my heart that we would end up being together.

I knew that getting into a relationship was risky for me. I had to question myself around my feelings for Patrick. Was it me or my addiction? Was I just afraid of being on my own? Was I running from something? I knew the meaning now of being left on my own. And it didn't frighten me any more. I knew in my heart of hearts that my feelings for Patrick were solid, that I wasn't looking for him to replace the drugs or to fill the void. I entered a relationship with Patrick with my eyes wide open.

———

When I left Keltoi to live on my own I became really friendly with Alison, the girl from Sky News. At first I was a little bit surprised that she wanted to be my friend. I was a recovering drug-addict and she was a reporter/journalist. Not a likely mix. And I thought that she would be too concerned about what other people thought. But she wasn't. When the drugs were taken away, we had much in common. The difference between us was that I coped with my life by using drugs. She coped by working every hour that

God sent her. She reminded me so much of my old friend Katie from Ballymun whom I hadn't seen in years, and I felt that I could trust her with anything. Spending time with Alison was making me realise that it wasn't only addicts who wanted to dull their pain. It was human nature. This was a bit of a revelation to me. I had been convinced that addicts were only half human. Like we were missing something. But the more I got to know Alison, the more I realised that she suffered from the same fears, the same anxieties and the same self-doubt as I did. We all do. But everyone deals with things in different ways. This information was a big relief for me. And for the first time in my life I felt connected to the human race.

Things were going so well that I was beginning to think something was wrong, but I wouldn't allow myself to be negative. I was training myself now to think positive thoughts. Even when I heard people talk about me on the streets saying, 'There's your woman with the arms', or nasty comments like 'You shouldn't have used drugs in the first place,' I wouldn't let it get me down. Some people lacked understanding, that was all. I had to take the good with the bad, and the majority of people were surprisingly supportive.

It was summer time. The sun was shining, I was clean and free from drugs and I had a roof over my head. That was the most important thing. Myself and Rachel were lapping up the sun, going shopping and having our own little parties on her rooftop. We were having the time of our lives. Patrick's music career was beginning to take off. He had been offered a deal to make six singles. All of us were chuffed for Patrick. We knew how much his music meant to him. And there was no doubt that he had a raw gift. My relationship with Patrick was my little piece of heaven. I was really beginning to think that I could easily spend the rest of my life with him. We had been together for six months now. Six months clean had always being a dodgy time for me in the past. For some reason I could never get beyond this stage. But things were actually going really well. My family loved Patrick the minute they met him. Especially Philip. He looked at Patrick as if he were God and he was amazed by Patrick's musical abilities. It wasn't long before they became really good friends. I was surprised that my grandmother approved of Patrick. She never liked any of the company that I kept and in her eyes no-one was ever good enough for me. But she saw something in Patrick that she really took to.

———

I noticed that I had missed my period. At first I didn't think much of it. My body was still adjusting to being clean. One week passed, two, then three. Now I was worried. Patrick came with me to get the pregnancy test and I nearly passed out when it read positive. This couldn't be right, I thought. I was convinced that I couldn't have children. I had done too much damage to my body. I couldn't be pregnant. It just wasn't possible. Six months ago I was at death's door and now I was pregnant. Patrick went white when I told him. And he stayed white for a couple of weeks. He told me that he wasn't ready for a baby. *We* weren't ready for a baby. We were too early in recovery for such a big responsibility. He was right, it would be a huge responsibility. But I wasn't about to run from it. Patrick told me that he would support me in whatever decision I made. And I decided to keep the baby.

My mother and my grandmother cried when I told them the news. They never thought that they would see the day when I would be pregnant. My grandfather, being my grandfather, showed no emotion when he heard the news. 'D'ye not think you're rushing into things a bit too soon?' he said. 'Would you not give yourself a chance to go to college first before you start having a load of babies?' But I knew that my grandfather was secretly delighted for me. I loved John dearly. His problems and his drinking had caused a lot of damage, but I didn't hold any resentment or hard feelings towards him, and I always knew where I stood with him. He never minced his words and neither did I—I had always stood up to him and he respected me for this.

For the first six weeks of the pregnancy I was in a daze. I just couldn't get my head around it, but I knew that I was happy. Then one day Patrick rang me. There was something different about his voice. He told me that he had something that he wanted to tell me. But he didn't have to tell me. I knew exactly what it was. He had used drugs.

I went to meet Patrick and I prayed to God that I was wrong. But the minute I saw his eyes, I realised I was right. Even though I knew that one of us could have a relapse, I still had big hopes that we wouldn't. I was heartbroken. I understood how hard it was to stop using once the cycle had been started. The dilemma I faced now was to either walk away from Patrick or to stand by him until he got strong again. It wasn't a difficult decision for me to make. I loved him dearly and I was carrying his child. I wasn't going to give up on him that quickly. But this would be dangerous for me, I knew that. I was putting my recovery at risk by standing by him. He told me that he didn't want to go back using drugs and that he would do everything possible to get himself back on the right road. I was under no illusion that I could carry Patrick or save him. Sure, nobody could save me. So I held my breath and I prayed to God that Patrick would save himself.

Within a few months Patrick had lost his apartment in transitional housing. He was no longer in his day programme, his music deal had gone down the drain and he was in the middle of a full-blown relapse. I was still completely drug-free and standing by him the best way I could, but protecting myself from Patrick's addiction was the most important thing. I topped up on my meetings, stayed around my friends and continued to go to my after-care in Keltoi, but everyone around me was getting worried. 'Patrick is a lovely fella, but you have to let him go,' they said. 'If he wants to use drugs, then that's his choice.' But I just couldn't walk away from him. My heart wouldn't allow me to. How could I just leave someone I loved when he was crying out for help?

So I ended up doing the opposite to what everyone told me to do. I moved into a flat with Patrick in the hope that this would help him to get clean. He did, but only for a couple of weeks. I was devastated by Patrick's relapse. I stood by and watched as Patrick continued to destroy himself. The Patrick I had met in Keltoi was quickly being replaced by addict man. I lived with Patrick for five months while he was actively using drugs. He somehow managed to keep it all away from me, but I didn't need to see Patrick using drugs to be weakened by his addiction. I had learned from experience that addiction was stronger than me and it was already beginning to show its ugly little head again. By now I was heavily pregnant and the thoughts of being a single mother really frightened me. I tried to keep myself occupied by achieving my goals and starting college, but it was only a matter of time before thoughts of using drugs entered my mind. I couldn't go back using drugs. I remembered people telling me that pain had no memory and this had been true for me every other time I had been clean. But not this time round: I vividly remembered the loneliness and desperation of my last relapse. I remembered the promise that I had made to myself to never give anyone or anything that power over me to make me go back using drugs. Patrick was far from ready to stop using. He was beyond human aid and it was something that I just had to accept.

———

On 13 March 2008, I gave birth by caesarean section to a beautiful baby boy. I had been in labour for twenty-three hours and at the time it felt worse than my whole addiction put together. Nobody had told me that giving birth could be so traumatic. Patrick was by my side through it all. He was adamant that his addiction wouldn't stop him from witnessing the birth of his baby boy. I had been knocked out with gas through the labour, and by the time I got to see our baby Patrick had him bathed and dressed. My mother, my grandmother and Philip were also there proudly looking on. Laying my eyes on our baby was the most magical moment of my life. He was so tiny and perfect and he had come from *me*. I couldn't believe it.

All my fears about whether or not I could cope with being a mother disappeared into the air. Myself and Senán bonded straight away. He was my little angel and everything I had been through was worth it just to see his beautiful little face. That night as I lay with Senán in my arms I thought about my life and all that had happened. I had been to hell and back again. I thought about my own mother and father and their inability to be there for me and to give me the love and stability that I needed. My heart broke at the thought of Senán going through the same thing. I held Senán as close to me as I could and I promised him that I would always be there for him. I wouldn't make the same mistakes that my mother and father had made. I would never abandon him.

But I felt so sad thinking of him growing up without a daddy. Patrick's using was completely out of control now, I knew that he was devastated about his relapse and his inability to be there one hundred percent for myself and Senán. He didn't seem to have much more fight left in him and I knew that now was the time I would have to walk away. Leaving Patrick was one of the hardest things I ever had to do. I felt as though I were going to die and I cried until I couldn't cry any more. But it wasn't about what *I* wanted now. It was about what was best for our son.

I knew in my heart that Patrick adored Senán and that he would never do anything to hurt him in any way. But I wasn't dealing with Patrick any more. I was dealing with his addiction, and his addiction couldn't be trusted. The same way my addiction couldn't be trusted when I was active. I was getting to see addiction now from the other side of the fence. I was getting to see it through my family's eyes. Watching Patrick destroy himself was like watching myself all over again, but without any drugs to numb the pain.

I moved in with my mother and Philip. My mother was a huge support to me around this time. She was my voice of reason. Every part of me wanted to run back to Patrick, but she gently reminded me that I had a child now and I had to put him first. The neck of her, I thought to myself. Who does she think she is, giving me advice on being a mother? Living with my mother now wasn't easy, but I reminded myself that the past was over and my mother was doing her best to be there for me.

Although I had removed myself physically from Patrick, I still wanted him to have contact with Senán. Drug addict or no, Patrick would still know his son and Senán would know his daddy. It was important for them both. Even though he was actively using drugs, he was great with Senán. But it was gut-wrenching watching them spend time together. They adored each other. Patrick would sing to him, as I stood there, not knowing whether to strangle him or wrap my arms around him. His addiction had ruined everything. But I knew that he felt worse about it than I did. He was homeless now, living on the streets and suffering so much because he had made that one mistake, using heroin. In spite of everything, my heart was very much with Patrick.

———

More than two years have passed since I put a drug or a drink into my body and people tell me that I am a totally different person now to the woman I once was. The wounds on my arms have healed although the scars are there to remind me every day. I've been told that the hepatitis C is no longer detectable in my body.

It amazes me to think that I put myself through all that and nearly killed myself in the process, all because I was afraid to feel. Now I know that the only way to get through something is to go through it. I have been through a lot and sometimes when I'm down I grieve my losses, but I don't give the negative thoughts any power. I no longer act impulsively. I know that no matter how strong the urge is to do something, that doesn't mean I have to do it. I am bigger than my feelings and my thoughts. Everything passes and I still have hope.

I no longer look for other people or things to fix me. It would be easy to do that, but how I feel about myself doesn't depend on what others think of me. These days, I try to look deep within myself for that higher part of me that is tenacious, considerate of others, gentle and understanding. I no longer believe that I am a bad person.

But I know that if I hadn't experienced all that I have done, I wouldn't be the person that I am today. I have been given a second chance at life and the opportunity to heal the damage that I have done. This applies particularly to my family. I have come to the conclusion that even if my mother had been there for me and none of what happened to me had happened, I would probably still have ended up on heroin. There were many factors which contributed to my becoming an addict, but I don't blame my family any more.

My relationship with my mother isn't perfect, but we are on the right road. Having a child of my own has made me understand more how difficult it is to be a good parent. My mother has admitted that she has made mistakes and she spends most of her time trying to make up for lost time. We are still learning to communicate with each other and we are both learning to forgive.

My uncle Laurence has never really got over the damage that my addiction caused: he was very close to it all, ferrying me to Cuba and back and living at home whilst I was going through the worst of it. But it seems that the longer I stay clean, the more he is beginning to trust me. The rest of my family are simply happy to see me alive, drug-free and still half intact. Especially my grandmother. She is my rock and someone whose love I am eternally grateful for.

Along the road of my recovery I have also been given the chance to mend fences with old friends. I bumped into my old friend Katie one day when I was visiting my grandparents in Ballymun. She still looked exactly the same. At first I just walked past her, giving her a nervous hello. But I knew in my heart that I had to apologise for any harm I had caused her. And I had caused her harm, using her identity on one occasion when I had been arrested for shop-lifting. When I hadn't turned up in court, a bench warrant was issued to her address. Katie had to go to court in order to sort it all out.

Nonetheless, I decided to approach Katie and say all that I needed to say to her. Katie told me that she wasn't one bit happy about being brought to court, but she was delighted to see me doing so well. She went on to tell me about how guilty she felt when I started to use drugs and she couldn't hang around with me any more. She had blamed herself and she had thought about me a lot over the years. Within a few minutes myself and Katie were laughing and joking about the good old days in Sillogue. It was as though it was only yesterday when we had all sat around on crates, smoking hash and listening to Bob Marley. Since then myself and Katie have stayed in contact and we have become good friends again.

When I started college I was shocked to discover that my old NA sponsor, Katriona, was my psychology lecturer. As soon as we got the chance to be alone, we had a good little cry over everything that had happened. We were laughing and crying at the same time and Katriona was only too happy to offer to be my sponsor again. But I got a real blast from my past when I ran into Derek one day in town. I couldn't believe my eyes. He looked like a different person. I had heard that he was clean, but I wasn't sure if this was true. At first we both just said hello. But after bumping into him time after time, we ended up having a chat. He told me that he was drug-free. He was studying in college and he was trying to make a better life for himself. He told me that he was haunted by memories of his addiction and of the hard time he had given me: he would have to live with those memories for the rest of his life and he was truly sorry. I needed to say sorry, too: for all the harm that I had caused Derek, because I knew in my heart that I had. I knew by him that he was still scarred by it all and so was I. But I was happy in the knowledge that we had both made our peace and now we could really move on.

Big Mick, my partner and mentor, had died four years before my recovery and I had been devastated at the time. But it was only now that I realised just what a role he had played in my recovery. When he died, I felt guilty that I couldn't be there after all he'd done for me and guilty that I hadn't made my peace with him fully. Apart from my grandmother, Big Mick was the one person who always believed in me and never gave up on me. He wanted nothing more than to see me get clean and stay clean. I never got the chance to show him how grateful I was. But I know that he is there in some way, watching over me still.

The one person with whom I haven't been able to build bridges is my father, perhaps because we never had a real relationship in the first place, but I met him not so long ago and we talked. I wanted closure and to hear in his own words why he wasn't there when I was a child. I was expecting him to point the finger at others, but he took full responsibility: 'I couldn't be there for personal reasons and I had to abide by that,' he told me, no doubt referring to the barring order which my family took out against him and which I knew about. 'But I always thought about you and wanted to see you. I'm here for you now,' he finished. But this wasn't enough for me—isn't enough. Too much damage has been done.

One person who reminds me how far I've come is my friend

Neil. It broke my heart to leave him behind in active addiction, and I wasn't willing to walk away without trying to help him first. He got clean not so long after me and he now lives in India with his mother. We are still best friends and he never lets me forget where I'm coming from. I've also made some really good friends since coming clean. My friend Chris made his way back from his relapse and he spends most of his time travelling the world trying to spread the message of recovery. He is still one of my most trusted friends. Myself and Declan are still very close. He is now a qualified psychotherapist who works with active drug users and is someone I am blessed to have as a friend. But I have yet to meet anyone like Patrick. All through his addiction I still loved him dearly. I tried to help him in any way that I could but without putting myself in danger. I can never take from Patrick the love that he has for his son or the encouragement that he always gave me to keep moving forward even though he was stuck with the drugs. I still love and cherish him and always will.

After a long battle with his addiction, Patrick is now drug-free and on the road to recovery. He has crawled his way back from active addiction and is living with his sister, who was one of my biggest supports all through Patrick's relapse. She knew exactly what I was going through and she was always there to let me know that I was never alone.

I am now in college studying psychotherapy and counselling and working towards getting a degree. I have no idea what I would like to do in the future, but it involves giving back in some form or another. Going into schools and giving talks to children about the dangers of drugs is something that I do regularly. I find this work to be so rewarding. I still have a strong feeling of loyalty towards NA and I attend meetings almost every week. If not for myself, then for others. NA has taught me almost everything I know. And the most important thing I try to implement in my life is the constant thought of others. It's not always easy when you have spent fourteen years thinking about nobody but yourself.

But I try my best. Having a baby doesn't give me the leisure to be selfish. And I thank God for this. Senán is the most precious, beautiful gift that I have ever been given and most days he keeps me going. In the beginning of my recovery doing the right things was alien to me. But now, after going against the grain every day, doing the right things is mostly instinctive for me. I have learned the hard way that addiction has nothing to do with the drugs. It is something that is still with me even now and I can never underestimate its power. The day that I stop being true to myself will be the day that I go back using drugs. Every day I do my best to apply spiritual principles to my life: acceptance, honesty, faith and lots of laughter. For now, I can safely say that I am living a life beyond my wildest dreams.

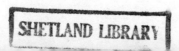

CONTACTS

Cenacolo Community, tel 094 9388 286,
email cenacolocommunityireland@yahoo.ie

Coolmine Therapeutic Community, Headquarters, Coolmine House,
19 Lord Edward Street, Dublin 1, tel 01 679 4822,
email declanarthur@gmail.com, www.coolmine.ie

Cuan Dara, Drug Detoxification Unit, Cherry Orchard Hospital,
Ballyfermot, Dublin 10, tel 620 6050, fax 623 5835

Keltoi, St Mary's Hospital, Phoenix Park, Dublin 20, tel 01 620 0040

Peter McVerry Trust, Head Office, 29 Mountjoy Square, Dublin 1,
tel 01 823 0776, fax 01 823 0778, email info@pmvtrust.ie, www.pmvtrust.ie

Rutland Centre, Knocklyon Road, Templeogue, Dublin 16, tel 01 494 6358,
fax 01 494 6444, email info@rutlandcentre.ie, www.rutlandcentre.ie

Soilse, 1–2 Henrietta Place, off North King Street, Dublin 1, tel 872 4922,
fax 872 4891, email soilsehp@hse.ie

Victory Outreach, Unit 11/12 Westlink Industrial Estate, Kylemore Road,
Ballyfermot, Dublin 10, tel 01 623 9383, fax 623 9390,
email admin@victoryoutreachdublin.ie, www.victoryoutreachdublin.ie